S0-EVQ-603

Recipes
Compiled By

The Independent Restaurant Association
1 East Park Avenue
Havertown, PA 19083
1st Edition, November 1994
ISBN # 0-9629776-1-6

Published by:
The Independent Restaurant Association
1 East Park Ave.
Havertown, PA 19083

TX
715
.R23
v.2

WIDENER UNIVERSITY
WOLFGRAM
LIBRARY
CHESTER, PA

DISCARDED
WIDENER UNIVERSIT

Publication 18534

Dear Reader -

It's time for another edition of the Head Chef's Recipes cookbook featuring hundreds of additional recipes from our Master Chefs who prepare these same dishes at some of the finest restaurants in eastern Pennsylvania.

As in our last edition of Head Chef's Recipes, these award-winning recipes include the personal trade secrets of each chef. These valuable tips can turn ordinary, everyday cooking into the same type of culinary "magic" that is usually found only coming from the hands of a renowned "Master Chef."

After trying these dishes at home, you might want to experience the original dish as prepared by the Master Chef who created it. Look no further than the back of the book where you'll find a complete list of the addresses and phone numbers of the restaurants where these dishes are regularly served.

We also invite you to use the many valuable coupons located just after the Restaurant Listings. The coupons are conveniently printed on the back of their respective ads. With these coupons, you can save money as you dine your way through our famous restaurants and experience firsthand the joy and gratification that an evening of fine dining can bring.

Bon Appetit!

Doc Loughran, President
Independent Restaurant Association

Special Thanks from Our Staff:
Maureen McLaughlin - Vice President
Jack Ryan - Vice President of Marketing
Elaine H. Oglesby - Assistant to the Publisher
Floyd Murray - Editor

Restaurants and Chefs - Alphabetical Order - As of 9/7/94

Proprietor/Head Chef Michel Wakim
Proprietor/Head Chef George Wakim
Chef Maroun Aboud
Aldar Bistro

_____

Executive Head Chef James E. Webb
Pastry Chef Guy Angelo Sileo
American Bistro Restaurant and Grill

_____

Proprietor/Head Chef Bobby Keough
Chef Bob Donovan
Chef Cory Lutterman
Sous Chef Norman Whitefield
Bobby's Seafood Restaurant

_____

Executive Chef Allan Vanesko
Bravo Bistro/Restaurant Passerelle

_____

Head Chef Dominic Ventura
Sous Chef Jeanne Sarne
Pastry Chef Gloria Elana Ventura
Cafe Elana

_____

Executive Head Chef Marco Carrozza
Chef De Cuisine Tom Downing
Cafe Nola

_____

Chef Hugh Moran
Central Bar and Grille

_____

Proprietor/Head Chef Scott Nyman
Chef Geoff Young
Dugal's Inn

_____

Proprietor/Head Chef George Wakim
Proprietor/Head Chef Michel Wakim
Chef Larry E. Langley
Evviva

_____

Chef Adolph Funches
Fireside

_____

Head Chef Mark Van Horn
The Gaslight

_____

Proprietor/Head Chef Scott Perrine
The Ingleneuk Tea House & Catering

_____

Head Chef Jerry Gonzalez
Kathryn's Inn

_____

Executive Chef Donald Pasquella
The Lagoon Hotel, Restaurant & Nightclub _____

Proprietor Head Chef Michel Wakim
Chef Michael Klaumenzer
Marble's Restaurant & Bar

_____

Proprietor/Chef Siamak Masoudi
Chef Mark Chopko
O'Flagherty's Restaurant and Bar

_____

General Manager/Chef Charlie Mayer
Head Chef Matthew Thompson
Packy's Pub

_____

Executive Chef - Richard Hudson
Palumbo's Edgmont Inn

_____

Chef Bob Kellock
Pike Family Restaurant

_____

Executive Chef Jim Coleman
Sous Chef Thomas J. Harkins
Restaurant 210 at the Rittenhouse

_____

Sous Chef Steve Bledsoe
Restaurant Passerelle/Bravo Bistro

_____

Executive Chef Jim Coleman
Chef De Cuisine Guillermo A. Pernot
Restaurant Tree Tops at the Rittenhouse

_____

Chef Juan Llamuca
Riddle Ale House

_____

Proprietor/Head Chef Pat Buonadonna
Ristorante Bona Cucina

_____

Proprietor/Chef Rosario (Russ) Taraschi Jr.
Head Chef Akin Randle
Rosario's Restaurant and Tavern

_____

Proprietor/Head Chef Robert Rottensteiner
Head Chef John Schatz
Rose Tree Inn

_____

Proprietor/Chef George Rossi
Chef Chris Buonopane
Rossi's Town Inn

_____

Proprietor/Head Chef Joseph P. Kirkwood
Chef E. Robert Jackson
Scampi Ristorante Italiano - Drexel Hill

_____

Executive Chef John Birmingham
Banquet Chef John Marco
Pastry Chef Michelle Keller
Septembers Place

_____

Head Chef Michael Walters
Seven Stars Inn

_____

Proprietor/Executive Chef Jan Cohen
Chef Christine Neugebauer
Thyme Catering

_____

Proprietor/Head Chef David Iannucci
Towne Crier Inn

_____

Proprietor/Head Chefs John and Anthony Polselli
Head Chef Richard Day
Trieste Restaurant

_____

Executive Chef John Birmingham
Pastry Chef Mary M. Berrie
Tymes Square

_____

TABLE OF CONTENTS

Restaurant Listing and Coupons in back of index.

APPETIZERS

CHIVES

PERFECT PARTY PLEASERS

Cheese and fruit tasting is an easy, conversation-making way to entertain friends before dinner. Seasonal varieties of fruit include peaches, nectarines, sweet cherries, figs, grapes, apricots, pineapple, strawberries, plums and melons. Or try fruits such as papaya and mangoes. Dried fruits such as prunes and raisins also team nicely with cheese and fresh fruits.

Some cheese and fruit combinations: Cheddar, Provolone and Camembert with pineapple, grapes, pears and walnuts. Brie, Monterey Jack and Feta with tangerines, strawberries and dried prunes. Colby, Gjetost, Emmenthaler and Roquefort with apricots, pineapple and plums.

Remember, if cooking the cheese for your appetizers, that excessive heat and prolonged cooking turns it stringy and leathery. When making a sauce, stir in the cheese toward the end of cooking time just until totally melted.

To keep egg yolks from crumbling when slicing hard cooked eggs, wet the knife before each cut.

The pointed end of a beer can opener is an excellent tool for deveining shrimp.

Out of ginger ale? Mix equal parts of Coke and 7-Up.

Use styrofoam egg cartons as trays when you need extra ice cubes for parties.

If the carbonation fizzes out of your champagne, add one raisin to the bottle. The raisin won't affect the taste but its raw sugar will start the bubbling up again.

Christmas Starter, dinner or breakfast: Serve Cranberry Juice topped with lime sherbet.

You can use frozen dough to make flaky crusts for appetizers. Thaw, cut into desired shapes, put in filling, brush with butter, bake 10-15 minutes at 375 degrees. Fillings can be choppedup chicken, roast beef or any cooked seafood; or any cooked vegetables as mushrooms, broccoli, cauliflower.

Place bay leaves (which are never to be eaten) in a tea ball for easy removal from sauces (or stews).

For instant white sauce: blend together 1 c. soft butter and 1 c. flour. Spread in an ice cube tray, chill well, cut into 16 cubes before storing in a plastic bag in the freezer. For medium-thick sauce: drop 1 cube into 1 c. of milk and heat slowly, stirring as it thickens.

Store carton of cottage cheese upside down. It will keep twice as long.

Try a new spice for your appetizers in place of salt. Blend together 2½ tsp. each of paprika, dry mustard, garlic powder, 5 tsp. onion powder, ½ tsp. ground black pepper and ¼ tsp. celery seed. Put all in a shaker and pass up the salt.

BAKED CRAB EN CROUTE

8 oz. lump crab
4 oz. cream cheese
1 oz. chopped chives
1/4 c. chopped shallots
1 oz. Worcestershire sauce

1/2 oz. Tabasco
2 sheets puff pastry
2 egg yolks
1 oz. sweet butter

Saute shallots in butter until lightly browned. Add to cream cheese to soften. Lightly mix in rest of ingredients, set aside. Cut puff pastry in 2-inch squares. Fill center of pastry with crab mix, top with another piece of egg. Moisten pastry, crimp edges. Brush pastry with egg yolks. Bake in a 400 degree oven for 10-15 minutes.

Marble's Restaurant & Bar
Proprietor/Head Chef Michel Wakim
Chef Michael Klaumenzer

LOCAL GOAT CHEESE WITH HOMEMADE SEVEN GRAIN OLIVE CRACKERS

GOAT CHEESE PYLONS:

8 oz. local goat cheese
2 oz. cream cheese, at room
   temperature
4 tbsp. virgin olive oil

2 tbsp. mixed herbs (chives,
   tarragon, rosemary, parsley,
   thyme combination)
Salt and pepper to taste

Place cheeses and olive oil in a bowl and blend well. Add the herbs and mix lightly to distribute them.
Spoon cheese mixture onto parchment paper or plastic wrap. Roll about the size of a silver dollar and twist ends to seal. Refrigerate until ready to be used.

SEVEN GRAIN AND OLIVE CRACKERS:

10 oz. cake flour
1 tsp. salt
1/2 tsp. sugar
1 tsp. baking powder

1 1/4 c. heavy cream
1/2 c. seven grain mix
1/8 c. chopped dry cured black
   olives

Combine flour, salt, sugar and baking powder. Blend. Add enough cream to bind into a ball. Mix in the seven grain and olives to blend. Rest and chill the dough, roll 1/8 inch thick, prick with a fork and bake at 360 degrees until golden.

Tree Tops
Chef De Cuisine Guillermo A. Pernot
James Coleman, Executive Chef

CURED ATLANTIC SALMON (GRAVALOX)

1 side Atlantic salmon filet (skin on from a 4 to 6 lb. fish)
8 oz. kosher salt
8 oz. granulated sugar
3 oz. cracker black pepper
1 bunch fresh dill (optional)
2 oz. rosemary

Combine sugar, salt and pepper. Rough chop herbs. Spread sugar-salt mixture over dry filet. Sprinkle the herbs on both sides. Place filet on a rack to drain excess liquid and refrigerate to cure for 2 days. Take the filet from the curing process -- scrape off the residue and proceed to slicing procedure.

The Restaurant 210 at the Rittenhouse
Sous Chef Thomas J. Harkins
James Coleman, Executive Chef

MUSSELS MATTHEW

8 mussels, steamed, served on half shell
3 oz. Prosciutto ham, diced finely
1/2 tomato, diced finely
1 oz. clarified butter
1 tsp. minced garlic
1/4 lb. fresh cleaned spinach
2 oz. Mozzarella, minced fine

Saute spinach, garlic, tomatoes and ham in butter until spinach is cooked and shrinks. Fill mussels on half shell with mixture and top with Mozzarella. Place under broiler until golden brown and serve.

Packy's Pub
Head Chef Matthew Thompson

CHICKEN QUESADILLA

1 soft flour tortilla shell
2 oz. diced tomatoes
2 oz. chopped scallions
4 oz. sliced grilled chicken breast

4 oz. mixed grated Monterey
  Jack cheese
Salsa and sour cream for serving

Take tortilla shell and put half of ingredients on it evenly. Roll up and fold ends. Place on buttered oven-proof plate or pan. Put in 450 degree oven until tortilla browns. Remove from oven, cut in thirds and place on new plate. Place rest of ingredients on top of tortilla, cheese last. Heat until cheese melts and serve with sides of salsa and sour cream.

Packy's Pub
General Manager/Chef Charlie Mayer

STEAMED CLAMS BIANCO

1 dozen little neck clams, washed
  thoroughly
1 glove garlic, crushed
Pinch of oregano
Pinch of parsley

Pinch of red pepper seed
Pinch of black pepper
4 oz. chicken broth
2 oz. white wine
2 oz. whole butter

Place all ingredients in a pan. Cover and steam until all clams open and smell of white wine goes away! Serve with your favorite hot crusty bread or rolls or pour over your favorite pasta.

Scampi
Head Chef/Proprietor Joseph P. Kirkwood

ACADIAN B B Q SHRIMP

1 3/4 lb. sweet butter
1 1/2 c. seafood stock or clam
  juice
6 chopped garlic
5 bay leaves, minced
5 tsp. dried chopped rosemary
1 tsp. dried oregano

1 tsp. nutmeg
1 tsp. cayenne peppers
1 tbsp. paprika
1/2 c. ground black pepper
1/4 c. lemon juice
1 tsp. salt

Combine all ingredients and heat slowly on low flame to blend together, stirring occasionally. Set aside.

Place 2 pounds of 16-20 shrimp (in shell) into a large sauteed pan, ladle on enough butter mixture to just cover shrimp. Over a medium-high flame, cook shrimp while turning and stirring until firm. Distribute shrimp evenly to serving plates and ladle mixture over them. Garnish with lemon wedge and fresh rosemary and serve. Serves 8.

Cafe Nola
Executive Chef Marco Carrozza
Chef de Cuisine Tom Downing

CLAMS CASINO

1/4 lb. bacon, 1/4 inch diced
1 lg. onion, 1/4 inch diced
1 sm. green pepper, 1/4 inch diced
3 slices American cheese, 1/4 inch diced

1/2 tsp. lemon juice
1/4 tsp. Old Bay
18 clams, shucked on half shell

Over medium heat, saute bacon until golden brown. Add onions and saute until translucent. Turn heat to high and add green pepper. Stir constantly and cook for 1 minute. Drain off bacon fat. Cool, mix remaining ingredients to mixture. Stuff shucked clams with mixture. Preheat oven to 375 degrees and bake clams for 8 minutes. Serve with lemon wedges.

Dugal's Inn
Chef Geoff Young

BAKED GREEN HORN MUSSELS

16 green horn mussels
1 lb. Brie cheese
3/4 c. olive oil

1 tbsp. chopped fresh garlic
1 tbsp. chopped fresh basil
1/4 tsp. crushed red pepper

Combine oil, basil, garlic, pepper. Pour into mussels. Top with Brie. Put in baking pan and broil for 8 to 10 minutes.

Septembers Place
Executive Chef John Birmingham

COCONUT SHRIMP

8 lg. shrimp, peeled and deveined   2 c. frying oil

BATTER:

1 c. flour
1 tsp. baking powder
1/2 tsp. salt
1 tsp. vegetable oil

1 c. beer (the good stuff)
1/2 tsp. Tabasco
1/2 c. coconut

    Blend and sift dry ingredients. Make a well in center and pour in the liquids, stirring, then whip until smooth.
    In a saucepan, heat frying oil. Dredge shrimp in flour, dip into batter and fry for 5 minutes.

Septembers Place
Executive Chef John Birmingham

STUFFED ARTICHOKE HEARTS WITH GOAT CHEESE FLORENTINE

10 artichoke hearts
11 oz. goat cheese
1 lb. chopped spinach

2 tbsp. chopped garlic
1/4 c. sun dried tomato, diced
2 tbsp. chopped basil

    Combine goat cheese, spinach, garlic, sun-dried tomato, basil. Fill artichokes with mixture and bake at 350 degrees until golden brown. Serve with your marinara sauce. Serves 2.

Tymes Square
Executive Chef John Birmingham

MOZZARELLA CARROZA

1/2 c. flour
2 1/4 inch slice Mozzarella
   cheese

2 tbsp. butter

BATTER:

1 egg
1 tsp. fresh garlic, chopped
1/2 tsp. Dijon

1/4 tsp. chopped parsley
2 tsp. Parmesan cheese

Dredge Mozzarella in flour. Dip it in batter, saute it in butter until brown and serve it with your marinara sauce. Serves 2.

Tymes Square
Executive Chef John Birmingham

BOURSIN TOMATOES

2 lg. tomatoes, sliced half moon
8 oz. cream cheese
1/2 c. sour cream
1 c. salad oil
2 tbsp. oregano
1 tbsp. basil

1 tbsp. granulated garlic
1 tbsp. Worcestershire sauce
White bread, toasted, crust cut
    off, and cut in 4
2 tsp. fresh minced parsley

Prepare tomatoes by cutting in half moon. Mix marinade of oil and spices. Place tomato slices in pan of marinate and refrigerate overnight.

TOPPING:

Whip together cream cheese, sour cream with 1 tablespoon oregano, 1 tablespoon Worcestershire sauce. Place tomato slices on toasted bread and pipe on cheese mixture with small pastry bag. Top with pinch of chopped parsley.

Palumbo's Edgmont Inn
Executive Head Chef Richard Hudson

PEPPER APPETIZER

1 green pepper
1 red pepper
1 yellow pepper
2 tomatoes

2 onions
Salt
2 tbsp. olive oil
1/4 c. white vinegar

Remove core and seeds from peppers and slice lengthwise. Peel and slice tomatoes and onions. Heat olive oil in a large saucepan. Add peppers, tomatoes and onions, saute to taste, and simmer, covered, for 1 hour, stirring occasionally. Remove lid and add vinegar and simmer for 15 more minutes. Allow to cool, and chill in refrigerator before serving.

Trieste Restaurant
Head Chefs John and Anthony Polselli

CRAB STUFFED MUSHROOMS

2 lb. lg. mushroom caps, cleaned, stems removed
2 tbsp. plain, lowfat yogurt
1 lg. egg, beaten
1/4 tsp. seafood seasoning
2 tsp. parsley, finely chopped
1 tsp. Worcestershire sauce
1 1/2 tbsp. lemon juice
1/8 tsp. salt
1/2 lb. backfin crabmeat
Parmesan cheese
Paprika for sprinkling

Arrange the mushroom caps in a shallow casserole dish. In a medium bowl, mix together the remaining ingredients and gently fold in crabmeat. Stuff each mushroom cap, forming a mound of stuffing 1/2 inch over the top of the mushroom. Sprinkle with Parmesan cheese and paprika. Preheat oven to 425 degrees and bake for 8 to 10 minutes. Yield: 6 servings.

Trieste Restaurant
Head Chef Richard Day

HERBED MOZZARELLA

1 lb. fresh whole milk Mozzarella, cut into 1-inch cubes
1/2 tsp. coarsely ground black pepper
1 tsp. coarse salt (kosher)
1/2 c. extra virgin olive oil
1/2 tsp. dried oregano
1/2 tsp. dried rosemary
1/4 tsp. crushed hot red pepper
1 tsp. dried thyme

In a medium bowl, combine all the ingredients. Toss to coat evenly. Cover and refrigerate for up to 2 weeks, tossing occasionally. Let return to room temperature before using. Yield: 16 to 20 pieces.

Trieste Restaurant
Head Chef Richard Day

ASIAN DUCK TACOS

2 stalks bok choy, julienned
1/2 tsp. ginger, minced
1 med. carrot, julienned
3 scallions, sliced

1/2 c. bean sprouts
1 c. shredded, roast duck meat
8 (6 inch) flour tortillas
3 tbsp. hoisin sauce

Mix all vegetables with ginger and duck meat. Spread each tortilla with hoisin on one side. Fill tortilla with vegetables and duck, fold over and bake until warm and crisp on the outside. Serve with Tomato Coriander salsa. 2 tortillas per portion.

TOMATO CORIANDER SALSA

1 c. chopped tomato
1 tsp. chopped ginger, minced fine
2 stalks, sliced scallions

1/2 minced jalapeno pepper
8 sprigs chopped coriander leaf
Juice of 1 lime
Salt and pepper to taste

Combine all ingredients and adjust seasoning with salt and pepper to taste. 4 portions.

Central Bar and Grille
Chef Hugh Moran

MEDITERRANEAN SALAD

2 head Romaine, cut and cleaned
12 oz. lobster tail, poached off (cooked) and cut into chunks
12 lg. shrimp, poached off (cooked)
1 lb. jumbo lump crabmeat
2 c. croutons

2 c. creamy Caesar dressing
1 c. roasted peppers
8 pieces artichoke hearts, cut in half
1/4 c. pine nuts
1/4 c. grated Romano cheese

In large mixing bowl, add Romaine, lobster, shrimp, crabmeat, croutons, roasted peppers, artichoke hearts, pine nuts. Mix together and add Romano cheese and dressing to your desired wetness.

Lagoon
Executive Chef Donald Pasquella

POTATO AND LEEK AND RED ONION GOAT CHEESE SOUP

2 med. red onions
2 oz. shallots, minced
4 lg. leeks, rinsed and chopped
11 oz. goat cheese
6 lg. Russet potatoes

2 oz. garlic, minced
4 c. whipping cream
10 c. chicken broth
1/2 lb. butter

In heavy, large saucepan, melt butter over low heat. Add red onions, leeks, Russet potatoes. Simmer until tender. Add shallots, garlic, chicken broth, whipping cream and goat cheese. Simmer for 30 minutes. Add salt and pepper to taste. 10 servings.

Lagoon
Executive Chef Donald Pasquella

PENNE WITH ANDOUILLE SAUSAGE, SHRIMP AND MUSHROOMS

2 oz. garlic
2 tbsp. virgin olive oil
1/4 lb. mushrooms Portabella
2 oz. pine nuts
1/2 lb. andouille sausage, diced
1 lg. leek, chopped

6 U-15 shrimp, peeled and deveined
1 tomato, chopped fine
1/4 c. sherry
1/2 c. whipping cream
1/2 lb. penne, cooked al dente

In oiled hot skillet, place diced andouille sausage, stir and brown. Add leeks, shrimp, tomatoes, garlic, pine nuts; cook for 2 minutes. Add sherry, whipping cream. Cover with lid 2 minutes. Add penne, then add 4 oz. butter, stir and serve. 2 servings.

Lagoon
Executive Chef Donald Pasquella

BRUSCHETTA WITH SUN-DRIED TOMATO PESTO

1 loaf semolina bread
2 c. extra virgin olive oil
2 c. sun-dried tomatoes
1 c. fresh basil

1/2 c. locatelli cheese
1 c. hazel nuts
4 tbsp. fresh garlic
Fresh Mozzarella

Lightly coat 1-inch slices of semolina bread with 1/2 cup of olive oil. Broil until golden brown.

In food processor, blend remaining olive oil with sun-dried tomatoes, basil, locatelli cheese, hazel nuts and garlic until mixture is incorporated into an even blended paste. Spread toasted semolina with 1/2 inch of pesto and top with fresh Mozzarella. Broil until cheese melts. Serve warm. Serves 4.

Rossi's Town Inn
Executive Chef Chris Buonopane

SPINACH AGNOLLETTI CAPONATA

1 lb. spinach agnoletti, blanched
1 med. eggplant, skinned and
   cubed
3 fresh plum tomatoes, diced
1 med. Vidalia onion, julienned
2 tbsp. non-parel capers
1/4 tbsp. red pepper flakes

3 garlic cloves, crushed, minced
3 Italian frying peppers, cut into
   rings
1/4 c. virgin olive oil
1/4 c. red wine
Salt and pepper

Saute onions with garlic in olive oil until garlic begins to brown. Add tomatoes, eggplant, peppers, pepper flakes and red wine. Cook until eggplant is just tender.

In boiling pot, reheat agnocletti and toss with rest. Add salt and pepper to taste and capers just before serving. Serves 4 as an appetizer, 2 as an entree.

Rossi's Town Inn
Executive Chef Chris Buonopane

DEVILED CLAMS

1 green pepper, chopped
1 sm. onion, chopped
1/4 lb. butter
13 oz. chopped clams in juice
2 oz. clam base

1 tbsp. dried mustard
1/2 oz. Worcestershire
Cayenne pepper to taste
1/4 c. flour

Saute onion and pepper in butter. Add dried mustard, Worcestershire and flour to make roux. Keep on low heat so not to burn. Bring chopped clam and clam base to boil. Mix clam to roux and cook. Put in pan and let cool. After cool, scoop out 12 (2 oz.) portions, then bread and fry. Serve with tartar sauce.

Pike Family Restaurant
Chef Robert Kellock

MARINATED BUFFALO MOZZARELLA, FRESH TOMATOES TOPPED WITH GRILLED LOBSTER TAIL

MARINATE:

2 c. extra virgin olive oil
2 single garlic cloves, chopped
    fine
2 tbsp. finely chopped basil

1/2 tsp. cracked black pepper
1/8 c. balsamic vinegar
1/4 tsp. salt

4 ripe plum tomatoes
4 oz. fresh buffalo Mozzarella
    cheese

2 (3 oz.) lobster tails, cut in half,
    left in shell

Slice tomatoes and Mozzarella cheese equally 1/8 inch thick. Place in marinate for 3 to 4 hours.

Place lobster, meat side down, grill for 4 to 5 minutes. Arrange tomatoes and Mozzarella on plate consecutively, spoon over marinate for moistness. Artistically place lobster on plate.

Bobby's Seafood Restaurant
Chef Cory Lutterman

PENNE ALLA VODKA

1 lb. penne pasta
1 chopped sm. tomato
1/4 c. chopped onion
1 c. heavy cream
1 tsp. crushed red pepper
1 tbsp. grated Romano cheese

1 tbsp. butter
1 scallion, chopped
1 tsp. chopped garlic
2 tbsp. virgin oil
2 oz. pepper vodka
Salt and pepper to taste

Cook off pasta and set aside.
In saucepan, place oil, garlic, onion and tomato and scallions over medium heat. Add crushed pepper, lower heat and add vodka. Vodka will burn off, then add cream, cheese, butter and salt and pepper to taste and let sauce reduce. Toss in penne pasta and stir. Sprinkle more cheese on top. Serves 4-6 as appetizer.

Cafe Elana
Head Chef/Proprietor Dominic Ventura

CLAMS OREGANATTO

4 dozen little neck clams
1/2 c. clam juice
1/2 c. white wine
1/8 c. virgin oil
1/8 c. butter

1 tsp. crushed red pepper
1 tbsp. crushed garlic
1 tsp. oregano
Black pepper to taste

Steam clams in large saucepan with 1/2 cup fish or chicken stock or clam juice. Let steam until clams open, then splash with wine, butter, and oil. Also add all spices. Let simmer for about 1 minute. Finish with chopped fresh parsley. Serves 4.

Cafe Elana
Head Chef/Proprietor Dominic Ventura

BOW TIES WITH BACON, ONION, TOMATO

4 slices bacon, chopped fine
2 tbsp. olive oil
1 lg. onion, chopped
1/2 lb. bow tie pasta (farfalle)
1 tomato, chopped
1/4 c. water

1/4 tsp. hot pepper seeds and
    flakes
1/3 c. cilantro or parsley,
    chopped
1/4 c. Parmesan or Romano
    cheese

In deep skillet, cook bacon until crisp; transfer to bowl. Drain off fat from pan (except 1 tablespoon). Add oil and onion. Heat on moderate heat until golden.

In a pot, heat salted water until boiling. Add pasta and cook. While pasta is cooking, stir tomato into onion mixture with water, red pepper seeds and flakes and salt and pepper to taste. Simmer 5 minutes. Stir in parsley and bacon. Drain pasta well. Add pasta to sauce. Toss well with sauce, add cheese and toss again. Serves 2.

Kathryn's Inn
Head Chef Jerry Gonzalez

GRAVLAX WITH MUSTARD SAUCE

GRAVLAX:

1 (2 lb.) fresh fillet of
   Norwegian salmon, middle
   part only with all bones
   removed
1 1/2 c. salt

1 1/2 c. sugar
1 tbsp. cracked white
   peppercorns
2 bunches fresh dill

MUSTARD SAUCE:

4 tbsp. mustard
2 tbsp. red wine vinegar

3/4 c. vegetable oil
Chopped dill to taste

GARNISH:

Lemon wedges

Fresh dill

For the gravlax, mix salt, sugar and peppercorns in a bowl. Rub onto both sides of the salmon very well. Place the fillet on a stainless steel tray and cover with dill and wrap with plastic film. Store in the refrigerator to cure for 48 hours.

For the sauce, whisk mustard into vinegar and then whisk in oil and dill to taste.

To serve, remove salmon from cure. Rub off superflous salt and pat dry. Slice into thin slices. Arrange on plate with sauce and garnish with lemon wedge and dill. Serves 6.

Towne Crier Inn
Chef/Proprietor David Iannucci

SHRIMP SCAMPI

15 shrimp
2 tbsp. fresh garlic
1/4 c. chopped fresh parsley
Chopped salt to taste
Pepper to taste
Pinch of red pepper

Pinch of red pepper seed
Pinch of oregano
1 c. seasoned flour (with salt and
   pepper)
1 c. oil for cooking
Stock

Heat oil in saute pan. Dredge shrimp in seasoned flour. Place shrimp in hot oil. Add seasoning. Remove shrimp when done, and add stock to retard garlic from browning. Serve over toast.

Towne Crier Inn
Chef/Proprietor David Iannucci

CRABCAKE RELLENO

1 lb. lump crabmeat
4 Poblano chili peppers
1/2 c. diced bell pepper
1/2 c. chopped scallion
5 eggs
1/4 c. mayonnaise
1 tbsp. Tabasco
1 tbsp. Worcestershire
1/2 tsp. garlic, minced

Bread crumbs
Flour
Yellow or blue cornmeal
Tomato salsa
Guacamole
Sour cream
Monterey Jack cheese
Oil for frying

Roast peppers over gas flame until outside is completely charred. Place in container and cover with plastic wrap. Set aside.

Pick crab of any shell. Place in bowl, saute scallions and peppers and garlic. Add to crab, add Tabasco, Worcestershire, toss. Add 2 eggs and enough mayonnaise and bread crumbs so that mixture holds together but is not too wet. Season with salt and pepper and set aside.

Take peppers and under running water carefully peel charred outer skin, working carefully. Make a slit with a knife in one side of pepper. Carefully remove seeds. Stuff peppers with crab mixture, roll in flour, then in remaining beaten eggs and then into cornmeal. Place in 375 degree oil and fry until golden brown. Drain. Serve with guacamole, sour cream and salsa. Sprinkle with Monterey Jack cheese.

Bravo Bistro
Sous Chef Stephen Bledsoe

HONEY/SOY GLAZED CHICKEN WINGS

4 lb. chicken wings
3/4 c. honey
1/2 c. dry sherry
1/2 c. soy sauce
1/4 c. chicken stock
2 tbsp. fresh grated ginger
1 tbsp. garlic, minced

2 tbsp. cornstarch
2 tbsp. cold water
flour seasoned with salt and
    pepper
Peanut oil for frying
Scallions, minced

Combine honey, sherry, soy, stock, ginger and garlic in saucepan over medium heat. Bring mixture to a low boil. Combine cornstarch and water and whisk into saucepan. Lower heat and simmer for 5 minutes. Remove from heat. Heat oil to 375 degrees.

Toss chicken wings to coat in flour. Shake off excess. Place in oil and cook until golden and done inside. Remove and drain.

In bowl, toss hot wings in enough sauce to glaze. Garnish with scallions and serve.

Bravo Bistro
Sous Chef Stephen Bledsoe

STEAMED CLAMS WITH ADZUKI BEANS AND NORI PESTO

48 little neck clams
2 c. cooked adzuki beans (found
    in gourmet food stores or
    substitute white beans)
1 c. saki
1 tbsp. garlic, chopped

1/2 c. nori pesto
2 c. fish or chicken stock
2 tbsp. butter
Salt and pepper
Nori strips for garnish

In saucepan, add clams, saki, garlic, stock. Cover and steam until just opened. Add beans, pesto and heat through. Taste for salt and pepper and finish with butter. Serve in bowls garnished with dried nori strips.

NORI PESTO:

5 sheets nori
2 bunches parsley
1/4 c. toasted macadamia nuts

1/4 c. Parmesan cheese
Vegetable oil

Soak nori sheets in water until soft, drain. In blender, add nori, parsley tops only, nuts. Puree slowly, add enough oil to create a smooth but somewhat thick mixture at end. Add Parmesan, refrigerate until needed.

Bravo Bistro
Sous Chef Stephen Bledsoe

ROASTED EGGPLANT AND LOBSTER RAVIOLI

PASTA DOUGH:

1 1/2 c. flour
2 eggs
2 tbsp. olive oil

2 tbsp. cold water
Salt and pepper

2 eggs, beaten

FILLING:

5 eggplant, split lengthwise
1/4 c. roasted garlic
1 med. onion, diced
3 tbsp. fresh thyme
2 c. sour dough bread crumbs

2 c. chicken stock
1 c. fresh lobster, cooked and diced
2 tbsp. olive oil
Salt and pepper to taste

PASTA DOUGH: Combine flour and eggs and mix with dough hook of electric mixer at low speed; gradually add olive oil and water. Continue mixing until dough is smooth and has a silky texture. Season with salt and pepper. Let rest in refrigerator 4-6 hours. Then roll into thin sheets.

FILLING: Saute onion and garlic in olive oil until lightly brown. Set aside to cool. Slice eggplant, brush with olive oil and season. Place a sheet pan and roast in oven at 350 degrees until brown. Let cool. Remove meat and discard skin.

In a saucepot, combine eggplant, onion, garlic, thyme, bread crumbs and chicken stock. Simmer on low heat until thickened, stirring constantly. Add diced lobster meat, season with salt and pepper. Let cool using a ravioli mold, lay one sheet of pasta on top ravioli mold. Brush lightly with beaten egg.

Place 1 tablespoon of filling in each slotted spot of the mold. Place second sheet of pasta on top of filling and seal with a rolling pin. Unmold and separate ravioli. Cook in salted, boiling water for 3 to 4 minutes. Serve with desired sauce. Lobster-Chive Cream Sauce recommended. Serves 6.

Passerelle
Allan J. Vanesko, Executive Chef

CAJUN MUSHROOMS

3 lb. washed button mushrooms
1/2 lb. sweet butter
1 1/2 c. Worcestershire sauce

1/8 oz. Tabasco sauce
1 tsp. salt
1/2 c. ground black pepper

In large saucepan, melt butter and toss mushrooms over medium heat. Add remaining ingredients. Bring to simmer and cover. Stir frequently and do not let mushrooms stick to side of pan. Mushrooms are done when they are glazed with a heavy dark caramel color, about 1 hour. Serves 6.

Cafe Nola
Executive Chef Marco Carrozza
Chef De Cuisine Tom Downing

EGGPLANT MARINARA

1 eggplant, skin on, diced 1/2
    inch cubes
1 (14 oz.) can crushed Italian
    plum tomatoes
5 leaves fresh basil, julienned
2 cloves garlic, crushed

1 tbsp. fresh chopped parsley
Salt and pepper to taste
3 tbsp. extra virgin olive oil
1/2 c. chopped onion
Romano cheese to taste

In a large skillet, add oil, garlic and onions until garlic browns lightly. Add tomatoes, basil and parsley, salt and pepper to taste. Simmer for 20 minutes. Add eggplant, cook 10 minutes and serve immediately in your favorite casserole dish. Sprinkle top with Romano cheese to your liking.

Scampi
Head Chef Ernest Jackson

GRILLED EGGPLANT AND TOMATO SAUCE

2 sm. firm eggplant, cut into 1/4
    inch thick rounds
Salt to taste
1/2 c. extra virgin olive oil
3 med. size ripe but firm
    tomatoes, halved and
    squeezed to remove seeds
    and watery juices

3 to 4 tbsp. red wine vinegar
1 clove garlic
10 to 11 fresh basil leaves

Preheat grill on broiler. Place the eggplant slices in a large dish and sprinkle generously with salt. Let stand for 30 minutes to allow the salt to drain out bitter juices. Pat slices dry with paper towels. Brush the eggplant slices on both sides with olive oil and place on the hot grill or broiler. Cook until golden and a bit charred, 1 to 2 minutes, then turn over to cook on the other side.

Grill the tomatoes the same way, and remove when they are colored on both sides and a bit wilted, 1 to 2 minutes. Cut eggplant and tomatoes into medium size strips and place in salad bowl. Season with salt and olive oil, vinegar, garlic and basil. Toss well, leave at room temperature for 30 minutes before serving.

Scampi
Head Chef Joseph P. Kirkwood

CAPELLINI WITH TOMATO AND CREAM

1 (28 oz.) can Italian tomatoes
6 tbsp. butter, divided
8-10 fresh basil leaves
1/2 c. heavy cream
1/4 c. Parmesan cheese

1/4 c. Romano cheese
Salt and fresh ground pepper to
    taste
1 lb. imported capellini

Lift the tomatoes out of their juice and puree in food processor. Melt 4 tablespoons of butter over low heat in heavy medium skillet. Add tomato puree and basil. Cook over medium-high heat until tomato puree thickens. Add the cream and Parmesan and Romano cheese, and continue cooking until sauce is fairly thick. Add salt and pepper. Cook the pasta until al dente. Drain.

Toss pasta with remaining 2 tablespoons butter. Add the tomato-cream mixture and toss. Serve immediately. Pass the extra Parmesan cheese.

Scampi
Head Chef/Owner Joseph P. Kirkwood

PECAN SESAME CHICKEN TENDERS

24 chicken tenders	1 c. ground pecans
1 c. bread crumbs	1/2 c. sesame seeds

DIPPING SAUCE:

1/4 c. honey	1/4 c. horseradish
1/4 c. mustard	

3 eggs for eggwash	2 c. flour
2 c. milk for eggwash	2-3 c. vegetable oil

Combine bread crumbs, pecans, sesame seeds. Combine milk and eggs; mix well.

In a third bowl, put the flour. First, dip each tender in flour, then eggwash, then coat them evenly with bread crumb mix. Heat vegetable oil in a saute pan. Saute chicken golden or until done. Use medium heat. Drain well.

Combine honey, mustard and horseradish. Serve with chicken. 8 servings.

Thyme Catering
Christine Amarosa Neugebauer, C.W.C.

STUFFED CHERRY TOMATOES

20 cherry tomatoes	Salt and pepper
4 oz. fresh Mozzarella cheese	1/4 tsp. fresh garlic, chopped
1 oz. sun-dried tomato in oil	very fine
1 oz. fresh basil	20 tiny basil leaves

Shred or dice Mozzarella cheese fine. Julienne the sun-dried tomatoes and basil. Combine cheese, sun-dried tomatoes, basil, garlic salt and pepper. Add a small amount of sun-dried tomato oil to bind mixture.

Later, hollow out cherry tomato. Cut off a flat piece on the bottom. Fill with mixture. Top with a tiny basil leaf.

Thyme Catering
Christine Amarosa Neugebauer, C.W.C.

CRAB EN BOULE'

1 (12 oz.) can lump crabmeat
6 oz. Brie cheese

1 round boule' of pumpernickel
bread

Read this whole recipe first.
Check crab for shells. Slice excess skin from Brie cheese with a serrated knife. Cut the top off the boule making an incision down on an angle in order to hollow the boule. Make a thin lid for the boule; dice the remaining chunks of bread. Use for dipping into crab.
Layer the crab and Brie inside the boule. Put the lid on. Wrap in aluminum foil. Bake 20 minutes at 375 degrees. Arrange on a platter. Add crackers for dipping.

Thyme Catering
Christine Amarosa Neugebauer, C.W.C.

CHICKEN ROSEMARY

16 chicken tenders
1/2 lb. fettuccini, cooked al dente
1 lg. tomato, diced
1 tsp. garlic, crushed

1 tsp. rosemary
1/4 c. olive oil
Salt and pepper to taste

Saute chicken breast in olive oil. When 3/4 done, add remaining ingredients and toss until chicken is cooked through. Serves 4.

The Gas Light
Head Chef Mark Van Horn

FILET AMERICANA

10 oz. filet tips, 1/8 inch dice
1 lb. scallops
1/2 c. diced tomato
1 oz. sherry
2 c. heavy cream

4 oz. drawn butter
Salt and pepper to taste
1/2 lb. fettuccine, cooked al dente

Over medium heat, add filet tips and scallops to drawn butter; cook. When 3/4 done, add diced tomatoes; toss until scallops are thoroughly cooked. Add sherry and heavy cream. Reduce to proper consistency. Serve over fettuccine. Add salt and pepper to taste. Serves 6-8.

The Gas Light
Head Chef Mark Van Horn

JUAN'S SPICY WINGS

3 lb. chicken wings
1 tsp. chicken base
1 tsp. dry mustard
1 tsp. cayenne pepper
1 tsp. black pepper
1 tsp. flour

1 tsp. salt
1 tsp. cumin
1 tsp. paprika
1 tsp. garlic powder
1 tsp. onion powder
4 oz. oil

Put all ingredients on baking sheet. Mix well by hand and bake at 375 degrees for 20 minutes. Serve with celery, carrots and blue cheese dressing.

Riddle Ale House
Chef Juan Llamuca

COQUILLES ST. JAQUES MORNAY

10 oz. scallops
1 oz. butter
3 tbsp. lemon juice
1 oz. butter
2 oz. sliced mushrooms
1 shallot, chopped
2 oz. dry white wine

2 egg yolks
2 oz. heavy cream
8 oz. hot cream sauce*
Salt to taste
Pepper to taste
1 oz. Gruyere or Parmesan
    cheese

*CREAM SAUCE: Garlic, chicken stock thickened with flour and water.

Saute scallops in 1 oz. butter for 1 minute; add lemon juice. Remove scallops and place in coquilles (shells). Saute sliced mushrooms and shallot in remaining 1 oz. butter. Add wine and liquid from scallops. Reduce 1/3.

Incorporate blended cream and egg yolks (liason) into hot cream sauce, tempering the liason first. Blend hot sauce mixture into mushroom mixture. Season. Pour over scallops. Sprinkle with cheese. Brown under broiler or salamander.

Seven Stars Inn
Head Chef Michael Walters

BABA GHANOUG

1 lg. eggplant
1 tsp. salt
4 cloves garlic
2 tbsp. olive oil

1/4 c. fresh lemon juice
1/4 c. tahini
Fresh pomegranate seed for
    garnish

Grill the eggplant 20 to 30 minutes on all sides. Let cool off, then peel it and put in a strainer. Let the juice drain out. Then chop it and transfer the eggplant and the ingredients to a food processor, making a coarse puree. Transfer to a plate and garnish with pomegranate seeds and enjoy a delicious appetizer.

Aldar
Chef Bryant Edwards

APPETIZER OF SWEETBREAD RAVIOLI WITH RED PEPPER COULIS

FILLING:

1 lb. sweetbreads, cleaned and
    diced
1/2 shallot, diced
1 clove garlic

1/2 pkg. mixed fruit, dried
2 oz. peach schnapps
1/2 c. brown stock
Salt and pepper to taste

DOUGH:

2 c. flour
5 egg yolks
1 tbsp. olive oil
1 tbsp. white wine

1 tbsp. water
Eggwash
Pinch of salt

SAUCE:

3 red peppers, thoroughly
    cleaned (sweet bell)
1 white onion
1 c. chicken stock

1/2 c. white wine
2 cloves garlic
1 tarragon sprig

FILLING: Sear sweetbreads in sesame oil over medium heat. Add all remaining ingredients except for schnapps and brown stock. Cook for 5 minutes. Flame with schnapps, add brown stock and reduce until binding.

SAUCE: Add all ingredients together. Bring to a boil. Boil for 20 minutes. Let cool and puree in a Cuisinart. Strain through a fine sieve and reserve.

DOUGH: Combine the flour and salt on pastry board, making a well in the center. Place the egg yolks, olive oil and wine into the well and slowly knead into a smooth dough adding water as needed. Roll dough out very thin using a pasta machine and cut into 3-inch rounds.

GARNISH:

1 bunch chives, chopped

RAVIOLI: For the ravioli, brush bottom round with eggwash. Place 1 tablespoon of filling in center and top with second round. Seal edges. Cook ravioli in boiling water al dente.

ARRANGEMENT: To serve, dollop sauce on plate. Place raviolis around sauce and sprinkle with chives. Serves 12.

Rose Tree Inn
Head Chef John Schatz

EXTRA RECIPES

BREADS AND ROLLS

THYME

FRESH FROM THE OVEN

Water or milk (whole, skimmed, evaporated or reconstituted nonfat dry) are most often used for breads. Water makes the crust crisp, while milk produces a soft crust and a creamy-white crumb. The liquid must be at the correct temperature; if it is too hot, it will kill the yeast; if it is too cold, the dough will take longer to rise.

Many different kinds of fat (butter, margarine, shortening, salad oil or lard) can be added to bread dough to improve flavor and make the dough stretch more easily. The bread will have a tender crumb and stays soft longer.

Eggs added to a yeast dough add flavor, color and nutrition. They soften the crust and give the interior a fine crumb.

Do not try to speed up the yeast in bread dough by increasing the amount of flour, sweetener or salt, or by adding ingredients. These will only make the bread heavier.

To test the rising of yeast dough: The dough is doubled when two fingertips pressed ½ inch into it leaves dents that remain. If dents fill in quickly, let rise 15 minutes longer and test again.

Ways to glaze bread before baking are: for a dark, shiny glaze, brush on 1 beaten egg yolk. For a light shiny glaze, beat the whole egg or brush on melted butter or margarine. For shine with no color, brush on 1 egg white beaten with 1 tablespoon water.

How can I test the vitality of yeast? Just before using the yeast, mix some into one-quarter cup of lukewarm water that has been enriched with one-quarter teaspoon of sugar, the food for the yeast. If the yeast mixture does not start to bubble within five to ten minutes, your microorganisms are dead or enervated and will not leaven your dough or batter.

When baking bread, if tops brown too quickly, cover loosely with foil. To test for doneness - tap top of loaf lightly with your fingertips. If it sounds hollow and is well browned on top, the bread is ready. Remove loaves from pans immediately so bottoms don't become soggy; cool on wire racks.

If you roll out dough between 2 sheets of waxed paper, dab some water under the bottom sheet and it won't skid away.

All ingredients for bread making should be at room temperature. It's important to use the right size pan.

Bread stores in a cool, dry place best. It may be kept in the refrigerator but will go stale more quickly. Bread keeps in the freezer for 3 months if tightly wrapped and you make sure to press out as much air as possible.

ORANGE STRAWBERRY MUFFINS

2 1/4 c. flour
2 tsp. baking powder
1 tsp. baking soda
1/2 tsp. salt
3/4 c. sugar

1/2 c. milk
1/2 c. sour cream
1/3 c. vegetable oil
1 1/2 tbsp. orange zest
1 c. strawberry sauce

Butter and flour muffin pan. In large bowl, mix flour, baking powder, soda, and salt.

In separate bowl, mix remaining ingredients. Combine and mix thoroughly. Fill cups approximately 1/2 to 3/4 full and bake approximately 15 minutes.

The Gas Light
Head Chef Mark Van Horn

BAKER BRAIDED YEAST BREAD

7 1/2 c. all-purpose flour
2 pkg. active dry yeast
1/3 c. sugar
2 c. warm milk

1/2 c. melted butter
2 tsp. salt
1 egg yolk, beaten with 1 tsp.
water for glaze

Sift flour, place half of flour in a large mixing bowl. Make a well in the center. Add yeast and 1 teaspoon sugar to the well. Add milk and stir to dissolve yeast while working in a little flour. Sprinkle small amount of flour over yeast mixture.

Cover bowl. Place in a warm place for 10-15 minutes or until cracks appear in the layer of flour on the top. This means yeast is active. Beat the remaining sugar, butter and salt. Add to the bowl with 1 cup flour.

Beat vigorously with wooden spoon until smooth and well blended. Stir in enough flour until dough pulls from sides of bowl. Turn dough onto a lightly floured surface. Knead in enough flour until it is no longer sticky. Then combine to knead for 8-10 minutes. Dough should be smooth and elastic.

Lightly grease a clean bowl with butter. Place the dough in the bowl. Sprinkle flour on top. Cover with a towel, set aside in a warm place until double in bulk for 1 to 1 1/2 hours.

When dough is double in bulk, it is ready to be shaped and baked. Punch it down until all the air is gone, then cut it into 3 equal portions. Shape each piece into a long strand, about 22 inches.

Place each strand on a flat surface close to each other, join them at the top and pinch them together. Braid the bread about half way down and flip it over, then continue braiding. Pinch the ends and tuck them into the braid.

Brush with egg mixture and sprinkle with seeds, coarse salt, oats, etc. Preheat oven to 400 degrees. Place on a greased baking pan. Bake 25-30 minutes or until loaf sounds hollow when tapped on the top.

Septembers Place
Pastry Chef Michelle Keller

QUICK PUFF PASTRY

7 1/2 c. all-purpose flour   2 tsp. salt
7 sticks unsalted butter   1 2/3 c. water

Preheat oven to 425 degrees. Sift flour onto a work surface. Make a well in the center. Dice butter and place around the edge of the flour. Sprinkle butter with a little flour. Sprinkle salt in the well and pour in the water carefully.

With one hand, work as much flour and water together as possible without including any butter. Stir several times to make soft dough.

Work in butter until well incorporated, kneading to mix well. Pull out pastry into a rectangle. Roll front to back and left to right, making a quarter turn each time, make 4 turns. Bake in oven until golden brown.

Septembers Place
Pastry Chef Michelle Keller

CAKES AND COOKIES

CARDAMOM

EVERYBODY'S FAVORITES

To improve an inexpensive cake mix, add one tablespoon butter to the batter for a richer-tasting cake.

Discover baking with mayonnaise. Try substituting mayo as a shortening or oil - it blends easily, adds moistness and contributes toward a tender texture.

Throwaway Cake Plate - Save bottom cardboards from pizzas and cover with aluminum foil. Great if you are donating a cake or pie to a cake sale.

Dip spoon in hot water before measuring lard, butter, etc. - it will slip off the spoon more easily.

Put flour in a large salt shaker and use for dusting cake pans, meat, etc. It is less messy and doesn't waste flour.

For recipes using beaten egg whites, the eggs should be separated when cold and the whites allowed to come to room temperature (egg whites reach their highest volume if beaten at room temperature). Cream of tartar or sugar added to the egg whites will increase the stability of the foam...the sugar should be added a little at a time. Be careful not to overbeat egg whites or they will become stiff and dry, having lost their elasticity, and will almost certainly collapse as soon as heat is applied. Be sure beaters and bowl, etc. are completely free of oil - any trace of oil will prevent the egg whites to fluff up.

Don't grease cookie sheets or cookies will tend to spread too much. When baking several batches in succession, let sheets cool before placing more dough on them or the dough will soften and spread and finished cookies will be misshapen. If you don't have enough spare cookie sheets, use inverted baking pans.

Any recipe which says, "and add one egg," can be made better by separating the white and yolk. This white, when beaten separately, adds bubbles, tenderness and makes the finished product lighter. This is true for nearly all boxed items.

Child's Party: Push animal shaped cookie cutters lightly into icing. Fill depressed outlines with chocolate icing. ALSO - Fill ice cream cones (flat bottoms) with cake batter half full and bake. Decorate with icing topped with colored sugar.

If your layer cakes stick to the bottom of their pans, return them to a warm oven briefly. The layers will come out intact in just a short time.

For baking cakes, use shiny metal pans or pans with a non-stick finish. Avoid dull, dark or enamel pans which can cause uneven and excessive browning. If using glass or porcelain-coated aluminum pans, reduce the oven temperature 25 degrees F. If baking more than 1 at a time,  arrange the pans in the oven so that you get the best air flow - stagger them from one shelf to another, not one directly on top of another. And do not have a pan touching the walls of the oven or touching another pan. Good air flow is very important to proper baking. (This is true for trays of cookies also.)

Cakes & Cookies

WHITE CHOCOLATE ANGEL FOOD CAKE

(Served with Drunken Fresh Fruit)

CAKE:

1 1/2 c. powdered sugar
3/4 c. cake flour
6 oz. finely grated white
    chocolate
1 1/2 c. egg whites (about 12)

1 1/2 tsp. cream of tartar
1 c. granulated sugar
1/4 tsp. salt
3 c. orange sherbet, softened

Move oven rack to lowest position. Heat oven to 375 degrees. Sift together powdered sugar and flour. Beat egg whites and cream of tartar in large bowl on medium speed until foamy. Beat in granulated sugar, 2 tablespoons at a time, on high speed, adding salt with the last addition of sugar. Continue beating until stiff and glossy. Do not under beat.

Gently fold in white chocolate. Pour into 10-inch ungreased tube pan. Cook 30-35 minutes or until golden brown. Cool upside down on top of the next of a bottle 2 hours. Can be made a day ahead.

DRUNKEN FRUIT:

2 c. seasonal fresh fruit
    (strawberries, blueberries,
    pineapple, peaches, etc.)
1 1/2 oz. fruit brandy
    (blackberry, peach, etc.)

1 1/2 oz. Frangelico
4 oz. chopped dates for garnish

Marinate fruit for 15 minutes to 45 minutes in liquor, tossing occasionally. Slice 2 pieces of cake fairly thin, place at 45 degrees to each other. Top with 1/2 cup fruit and top with chopped dates. Serve with a side of vanilla ice cream, if desired.

O'Flagherty's
Chef Mark Chopko

RICOTTA CHEESE CAKE WITH RAISINS AND RUM

CRUST, PART I:

1/2 c. Crisco shortening
1/2 c. sugar
2 c. flour

1 tsp. baking powder
2 eggs

Mix together until firm. Then spread out with rolling pin between wax paper. Remove paper, take dough and form around sides and bottom of 10-inch spring pan.

BATTER MIX, PART II:

1/4 c. heavy cream
5 eggs
1 1/4 c. sugar
3 lb. ricotta cheese

2 tbsp. vanilla extract
Cinnamon to taste
1 c. raisins
2 oz. rum

In mixing bowl, take eggs and sugar; mix well. Add in vanilla extract, cinnamon and heavy cream; mix well. Add in ricotta and continue to mix for 3 minutes. Pour in raisins and rum and mix by hand. Pour mixture into prepared spring pan. Bake at 400 degrees for 15 minutes, then turn down oven to 350 degrees and bake for 1 1/2 hours.

Test with toothpick in center to see if completely boiled. If needed, bake 15 minutes more. When baking is complete, let cool, then refrigerate. Serve cold.

Cafe Elana
Head Chef/Proprietor Dominic Ventura

ELANA'S ANISE CAKE

6 lg. eggs
2 c. sugar
1 c. light oil
1 c. orange juice
1 tbsp. anise seeds (no stems)
1 tsp. lemon zest

1 tsp. lemon extract
1 tsp. anise extract
1 tbsp. pure vanilla extract
2 tbsp. 10X sugar
3 c. flour
1 tbsp. baking powder

In a 2-cup measuring bowl, add orange juice, lemon extract, anise extract and vanilla extract. Stir and set aside. Measure 3 cups flour and baking powder in sifter and sift.

In mixing bowl, add eggs and sugar; mix well. Add oil. Continue to mix. Add anise seed, lemon zest. Slowly add orange juice mixture. Blend well, slowly add sifted flour, 1 cup at a time, scraping bowl around as you mix. Beat for 5 minutes at medium speed.

Pour batter into a greased and floured tube pan. Bake at 350 degrees for 1 1/2 hours. After baking, set aside for 5 to 10 minutes, then separate tube pan and let cool. Sprinkle with powdered sugar.

Cafe Elana
Pastry Chef Gloria Elana Ventura

COCONUT BISCOTTI

8 eggs
2 1/2 c. sugar
8 oz. softened butter
2 tbsp. vanilla extract

1 1/2 tbsp. coconut extract
2 tbsp. baking powder
6-7 c. flour, sifted

In mixing bowl, beat butter until creamy. Add sugar, continue to beat. Add eggs, beat well. Add extracts, continue to beat. Slowly add in flour, 2 cups at a time, until dough is stiff. If mixer is not strong enough, remove from mixer and knead by hand until dough is stiff and smooth. Take dough and cut into 6 loaves. Roll out each loaf to flat long loaves by hand so 2 loaves will fit on a baking sheet.

On a greased and floured sheet, bake loaves for 15 to 20 minutes at 350 degrees or until golden and firm to the touch. Remove from oven and cut loaves into 1-inch slices while warm. Then let cool. After slices are cool, you may dribble them with icing or chocolate to personalize them to your taste.

Cafe Elana
Pastry Chef Gloria Elana Ventura

MOCHA RUM CAKE WITH 3 BERRY GLAZE

Cocoa powder
3 c. all-purpose flour
1 1/2 tsp. baking soda
3/4 tsp. salt
3/4 lb. chopped bittersweet
  chocolate
1 1/2 c. butter, cut into pieces
1 1/2 c. espresso
2 1/4 c. sugar
1/3 c. dark rum

3 eggs, beaten lightly
1 1/2 tsp. vanilla extract
Confectioners' sugar
Whipped cream
2 pt. raspberries
1 pt. strawberries
1 pt. boysenberries
2 c. water
1/4 c. sugar

Preheat oven to 300 degrees. Butter a 4 1/2 inch deep bundt pan and dust with cocoa powder.

In bowl, mix flour, baking soda and salt. In double boiler, melt chocolate and butter. Remove chocolate from heat and put in separate mixing bowl. Mix in rum, coffee and sugar with a mixer. Beat in flour a little at a time until completely incorporated. Beat in eggs and vanilla until mixed and pour into prepared pan. Bake cake in middle of oven until done, about 1 1/2 hours. Test with toothpick. Let cake cook completely and invert onto serving plate.

In saucepan, bring 2 cups water, 1/4 cup sugar to a boil and add berries. Cook for 10 minutes until mixture reduces by half. Let cool slightly and puree in food processor. Lace glaze over cake and chill. Serve with fresh whipped cream and confectioners' sugar.

Rossi's Town Inn
Executive Chef Chris Buonopane

CHOCOLATE CAKE

2 1/4 c. sifted cake flour
1 1/3 c. sugar
3 tsp. baking powder
1 tsp. salt
1/2 c. extra light olive oil
5 egg yolks

3/4 c. cold water
2 tsp. vanilla extract
1 c. egg whites (7 or 8)
1/2 tsp. cream of tartar
3 squares unsweetened
   chocolate, grated

Sift flour with sugar, baking powder and salt into mixing bowl. Make "hole" in center. Add olive oil, egg yolks, water and vanilla; then beat until smooth.

In separate bowl, beat egg whites and cream of tartar until very stiff, then fold in flour mixtures and grated chocolate. Pour mixture into ungreased 10-inch tube pan and bake at 325 degrees for 55 minutes. Raise temperature to 350 degrees and continue baking for 15 minutes or until top springs back to touch. Cool thoroughly. Remove to serving platter, garnish with powdered sugar and fresh raspberries.

Scampi
Head Chef/Owner Joseph P. Kirkwood

HERSHEY BAR CAKE

1/2 lb. butter
2 c. sugar
4 eggs
16 oz. Hershey's syrup
2 1/2 c. flour

1/2 tsp. baking soda
1/4 tsp. salt
1 c. sour cream
2 tsp. vanilla
1/2 lb. Hershey bar, melted

Cream sugar and butter. Add eggs, one at a time. Beat thoroughly. Add Hershey's syrup. Sift flour, salt and baking soda together. Add alternately with sour cream. Add vanilla and melted chocolate. Grease and flour tube pan. Bake at 325 degrees for 1 1/2 hours.

Seven Stars Inn
Head Chef Michael Walters

WHITE CHOCOLATE BROWNIE CHEESE CAKE

1/2 box instant brownie mix
2 lb. cream cheese
1 c. sugar
2 eggs, lightly beaten
2 tbsp. cornstarch

2 tbsp. vanilla
4 oz. white chocolate, melted
    over double boiler
1 c. sour cream

Butter and flour 10-inch springform pan. Prepare brownie mix according to directions. Layer 1/2 inch thick on bottom of pan. Bake until done. Cool.

In Kitchen Aid, cream together cream cheese and sugar. Beat in cornstarch, eggs and vanilla. Scraping down sides of bowl, add white chocolate and sour cream. Pour mixture into springform and bake at 250 degrees, rotating every 20 minutes until filling is firm to the touch approximately 1 1/2 hours.

NOTE: If top begins to crack or turn brown, reduce heat.

Remove from oven and cool on rack. Refrigerate overnight. Remove from pan, garnish and serve.

American Bistro
Pastry Chef Guy Angelo Sileo

EXTRA RECIPES

DESSERTS

MINT

DEFINITELY DESSERT

Fudge won't "sugar" if you add a dash of cream of tartar.

Soften "hard as a rock" brown sugar by placing a slice of soft bread or ½ an apple in the package and closing tightly. In a couple hours the brown sugar will be soft again.

Too much sugar in a recipe? Add a few drops of lemon juice or vinegar.

Use a pizza cutter to cut bars or bar-cookies into nice, smooth squares in half the time.

The more eggs yolks in doughnut dough, the less grease they will absorb when fried.

A few potato slices added to the oil will keep doughnuts from burning.

After mixing the dough for doughnuts, put in refrigerator at least 1 hour to make it easier to handle.

Sweetened condensed milk and evaporated milk are entirely different products and **cannot** be used interchangeably in recipes. Sweetened condensed milk is fresh, whole milk with 60% of the water removed and 45% cane sugar added (sugar acts as a preservative). Evaporated milk is whole milk from which water is removed but no sugar added. Sweetened condensed milk has a much thicker consistency and is great for desserts because it will not get "sugary" when heated and will not form ice crystals in frozen desserts. Also, it thickens without heat when combined with an acid such as lemon, orange, pineapple or apple juices.

If you are melting chocolate in a double boiler or a custard cup set in a pan of water, do not boil the water as this will only thicken or curdle the chocolate.

To keep granulated sugar from lumping, place a couple of salt crackers in container and cover tightly.

Before measuring honey or other syrup, oil the cup with cooking oil and rinse in hot water.

The key to successful custard preparation is low heat; high heat causes the eggs to curdle, resulting in lumpy, thin mixtures. Either cook custard in a double boiler or if cooking over direct heat, always use a heavy saucepan. Stir the mixture constantly with a whisk. Check thickness by lifting the spoon from custard and holding it for 15 to 20 seconds; if the spoon does not show through mixture, the custard has thickened to the correct consistency.

Desserts

WHITE CHOCOLATE MOUSSE

1 lb. white chocolate
1 qt. WAWA heavy whipping
  cream

1 oz. gelatin
1 c. milk

    In a double boiler, put white chocolate in small pieces. Add milk. Slowly melt, stir continuously. Whip the heavy cream stiff. Dilute gelatin in a little milk. When smooth, add to chocolate. Keep whipped cream very cold. Cool chocolate completely. Fold chocolate and whipped cream together. Pour into serving bowl. Refrigerate to set.

Thyme Catering
Christine Amarosa Neugebauer C.W.C.

GAS LIGHT RUM CAKE

1 c. chopped walnuts
1 c. butter or margarine
2 c. sugar
3 c. flour
3 tsp. baking powder

1/2 tsp. salt
4 eggs
1/2 c. milk
1/2 c. dark rum
1 tsp. vanilla

GLAZE:

1/4 lb. butter
1/4 c. water

1 c. sugar
1/2 c. rum

    CAKE: Heat oven to 325 degrees. Grease and flour 10-inch bundt pan. Spread chopped nuts over bottom of pan. Beat together softened butter and sugar until fluffy. Add eggs, one at a time. Beat well. Add flour, baking powder, and salt alternating with liquids.
    When well mixed and smooth, pour over nuts in pan and bake 1 hour. Cool cake and invert on dish or tray. Prick entire surface, then spoon glaze over.
    GLAZE: Combine first 3 ingredients in small pan and bring to boil. Cook 10 minutes. Remove from heat and add rum. Wrap in foil and refrigerate.

The Gas Light
Pastry Chef Mildred Lobb

JEWISH APPLE CAKE

5 cooking apples, pared and
    sliced
4 tsp. cinnamon
2 1/3 c. sugar
1 c. margarine
4 eggs

3 c. flour
3 tsp. baking powder
1/2 tsp. salt
1/3 c. orange juice
1 1/2 tsp. vanilla extract
1 tsp. almond extract

Mix apples with 1/3 cup sugar and cinnamon. In mixing bowl, combine butter and sugar and beat until fluffy. Add eggs, one at a time, and beat smooth. Mix flour, baking powder, and salt. Add to batter alternating with juice and extracts. Put small amount of batter in bottom of greased and floured bundt pan.

Arrange a layer of apples over batter, then layer of batter, then more apples and batter to complete. Bake at 350 degrees for 1 hour. Cool on wire rack and dust with powdered sugar.

The Gas Light
Pastry Chef Mildred Lobb

GOAT CHEESE WITH THREE NUT CRUST AND RASPBERRY CUMBERLAND SAUCE

1 lb. Boucheron cheese, shaped
    into 4 cakes
1/8 c. pine nuts
1/8 c. pistachios

1/8 c. almonds
Salt and pepper
2 eggs, beaten
1/4 c. flour

Grind nuts in a food processor. Season cheese with salt and pepper. Dredge in flour. Dip in egg and roll in nuts. Fry in peanut oil until golden.

SAUCE:

1/4 c. raspberry preserves,
    strained
1/4 c. red port wine
1 orange
1 lemon

1 lime
Pinch of crushed red pepper
Pinch of cayenne pepper
1/8 tsp. fresh chopped ginger
1 shallot, diced

In a saucepan, combine preserves, port wine and juice of orange, lemon, lime, red pepper, cayenne, ginger and shallot. Simmer 1/2 hour. Chill. Put sauce on plates, place cheese on top of sauce. Serve with fresh fruit.

American Bistro
Executive Head Chef James E. Webb

PECAN PIE

1/2 lb. butter, melted
6 eggs
2 tsp. vanilla
1 1/2 c. brown sugar

2 c. Karo syrup
2 pie shells
4 oz. pecans

Combine butter, eggs, vanilla and brown sugar and beat 3 minutes at high speed. Add Karo, beat 3 minutes. Pour in melted butter, beat 2 minutes more. Prebake shells in oven at 275 degrees until hot and dry. Add pecans. Fill with liquid. Bake 50 minutes at 375 degrees.

Seven Stars Inn
Head Chef Michael Walters

VANILLA CINNAMON TOASTED ALMOND ICE CREAM

24 egg yolks
4 c. sugar
4 c. milk
1 vanilla bean, split lengthwise

2 tbsp. cinnamon
1 c. slivered almonds
1 qt. heavy cream

In large saucepan, scald milk and 2 cups sugar. Scrape vanilla bean into milk. Do not boil.

In Kitchen Aid, whisk egg yolks and sugar until ribboned. Pour scalded milk into ribboned yolks. Remove to heavy bottomed stainless steel pot. Cook over medium heat until thick, stirring bottom constantly. (Thick enough when it coats the back of a spoon.) Work in cinnamon and cream. Cool. Freeze in ice cream maker. Serve with fruit berries.

American Bistro
Pastry Chef Guy Angelo Sileo

JUAN'S FAMOUS RICE PUDDING

1/2 gallon milk
1 lb. sugar
1 oz. vanilla
1/2 lb. rice
1 oz. cinnamon

6 oz. margarine
6 lg. eggs
1 c. heavy cream
1 qt. milk

Mix 1/2 gallon of milk, sugar, vanilla, rice and cinnamon. Bring to a boil on high heat. Turn temperature to low. After mixture boils, add 1 quart milk. Add margarine and cook on low heat for 1 hour. Stir frequently or until rice is soft. Beat eggs and heavy cream well and add to mixture. Mix well until custard forms. Simmer on low for about 5 minutes. Pour into shallow pan. Sprinkle with cinnamon and cool.

Riddle Ale House
Chef Juan Llamuca

POMPEI'S FAMOUS CHEESECAKE

2 lb. cream cheese, at room
    temperature
4 oz. margarine, at room
    temperature
2 oz. sour cream

1 oz. vanilla
2 c. sugar
5 lg. eggs
Pinch of cinnamon

Beat all ingredients except cinnamon and eggs. Add eggs, one at a time, and beat again. Thoroughly grease and flour springform pan. Pour mixture into pan, sprinkle with cinnamon. Place pan on sheet of aluminum foil, tuck edges of foil around pan. Use pan large enough for springform pan to sit in middle. Fill large pan to 3/4 of springform pan with hot water. Bake at 350 degrees in preheated oven for 2 1/2 hours. After first hour, cover with aluminum foil. Let cool for 3 hours. Loosen edges and serve.

Riddle Ale House
Chef Juan Llamuca

PISTACHIO ICE CREAM

4-inch piece of vanilla bean
1 c. half & half
2 c. whipping cream
2/3 c. sugar

6 egg yolks
1 c. chopped, toasted pistachio
    nuts
1/4 c. pistachio paste

Split the vanilla bean in half lengthwise and scrap the fine black seeds into a non-corroding saucepan. Add the vanilla bean pod, half & half, cream and sugar and warm the mixture, stirring occasionally, until the sugar has dissolved.

Whisk the egg yolks just enough to mix them and whisk in some of the hot half & half mixture. Return to the pan and cook over low heat, stirring constantly, until the custard coats the spoon (when you draw a finger across the custard coating the back of the spoon, your finger should leave a clear trail.)

Strain through a medium-fine strainer to remove any lumps that may have formed, scraping as much of the vanilla bean through the strainer as you can. Strain the custard into a storage container, recovering the vanilla bean pods from the strainer and putting them in the container to flavor the ice cream mixture while it chills.

Cover the container tightly and chill the custard thoroughly. When you are ready to freeze the mixture, remove the vanilla bean pods and add the chopped pistachios and paste. Freeze according to the directions for your ice cream maker.

Tree Tops
Chef De Cuisine Guillermo A. Pernot
James Coleman, Executive Chef

RIPE BANANA CREME CARAMEL

1 pt. milk	3 eggs
1/2 c. sugar	2 egg yolks
3 bananas, pureed	1 c. sugar
1/2 split vanilla bean	1/8 c. water

Steep and simmer the milk, sugar, banana puree and split vanilla bean for 10 minutes over low heat. Temper in the eggs and yolks to thicken slightly strain through a fine strainer and cool.

Melt sugar in water; cook to light caramel stage. Divide immediately into the 4 individual ramekin molds. Bake at 325 degrees in a water bath for 50 minutes or until it tests done. Chill fully and invert to unmold.

Tree Tops
Chef De Cuisine Guillermo A. Pernot
James Coleman, Executive Chef

CHOCOLATE MOUSSE

2 lb. semi-sweet chocolate	12 oz. unsalted butter

Melt together, cool to room temperature.

18 egg yolks	6 oz. liquor (your choice)
9 oz. sugar	1 1/2 qt. heavy cream

Whip to ribbon stage, thick and lemon colored.

1 1/2 qt. heavy cream, lightly whipped to soft peaks

Slowly fold chocolate mix into egg mixture, alternating with heavy cream.

In a large bowl, place the thickened egg yolk mixture. Whip in, by hand, the melted chocolate, then fold in the whipped cream gently to obtain a smooth mousse. This mixture can be flavored with any liquor added to the egg yolk mixture before the chocolate goes in. Roasted, chopped nuts, dry type fruits (not weeping out too much liquid) or chopped nut brittle will work very well.

Tree Tops
Chef De Cuisine Guillermo A. Pernot
James Coleman, Executive Chef

CHARDONNAY WINE CREAM CRUMPLE

8 sheets phyllo dough	1 oz. cornstarch
1 stick melted butter	12 egg yolks
1 pt. chardonnay wine	1/2 lemon, juiced
1 c. granulated sugar	1/2 stick butter

Bring the wine to a simmer. Combine the sugar, starch, egg yolks and lemon juice. Temper in and bring back to a boil to thicken, stirring constantly. Whisk in the butter to incorporate and cool completely.

Brush a sheet of phyllo lightly with melted butter. Repeat with three more sheets. Cut the dough in half. Repeat with the other 4 sheets. Cut them in half. Divide 1/4 of the cream between the four layered phyllo sheets. Fold up to seal, bake at 375 degrees until golden. Serves 4.

The Restaurant 210 at the Rittenhouse
Sous Chef Thomas J. Harkins
James Coleman, Executive Chef

RASPBERRY, PISTACHIO AND MILK CHOCOLATE BON BONS

1/2 pt. milk
4 oz. sugar
4 egg yolks
1 1/2 oz. cornstarch
8 sheets of phyllo dough

1 stick sweet butter, melted and cool
4 tbsp. pistachio paste
4 oz. milk chocolate drops
1/2 pt. fresh raspberries

TO MAKE PASTRY CREAM: Heat the milk to a simmer. Mix the sugar and cornstarch together, add the yolks and mix smooth. Slowly add 1 pint of hot milk to the sugar and yolk mixture. Whisk smooth; pour the yolk mixture into the milk and bring to a boil whisking constantly. Cool and add the pistachio paste.

TO ASSEMBLE: Lay a sheet of phyllo on a dry surface and lightly brush with the melted butter. Repeat with three more sheets. Cut the sheets in quarters and place 1 1/2 tablespoon of the pastry cream in the center. Top with a few berries and some chocolate chips. Crimp like a bon bon. Make all 8 pieces. Brush with butter and bake at 375 degrees for 8 to 10 minutes. Serve immediately with choice of ice cream. Serves 4.

The Restaurant 210 at the Rittenhouse
Sous Chef Thomas J. Harkins
James Coleman, Executive Chef

INGLENEUK HOMEMADE APPLE PIE

Your favorite pie crust dough
8 c. peeled, cored, and thinly sliced apples (Gravenstein, Jonathan, Pippin, or Granny Smith)
1 tbsp. lemon juice

1 c. sugar
3 tbsp. cornstarch or tapioca
1 1/2 tsp. ground cinnamon
1/4 tsp. ground ginger
2 tbsp. butter or margarine
Milk

Preheat oven to 425 degrees. Place apple slices in a large bowl. Sprinkle apples with lemon juice, sugar, cornstarch, cinnamon, and ginger; stir to blend well; set aside.

Place apples in pastry shell, mounding them a little in center. Pour in any remaining juice from bowl, then dot with butter. Roll out top crust, place over filling, and flute edge to seal. Brush top lightly with milk. To prevent excess browning of rim, wrap edge with a 2 to 3-inch wide strip of foil. Set pie on a rimmed baking sheet and bake on lowest rack of oven.

Bake for 30 minutes. Remove foil and continue to bake for 20 to 30 more minutes or until apples are fork-tender. Let cool on a rack. Serve warm or at room temperature; or refrigerate and serve cold. To reheat, warm pie, uncovered, in a 350 degree oven for 10 to 15 minutes. Makes 6 to 8 servings.

Ingleneuk Teahouse
Proprietor/Head Chef Scott Perrine

BAKED CUSTARD

2 c. milk
1/4 c. sugar
3 whole eggs or 6 egg yolks

1/2 tsp. vanilla
Ground nutmeg or ground
   cinnamon

In a pan over medium heat, scald milk (heat until small bubbles appear); remove from heat and stir in sugar until dissolved.

In a small bowl, beat eggs slightly. While constantly stirring, gradually pour milk mixture into eggs, then stir in vanilla. Pour into 5 or 6-oz. custard cups (or into a 1-quart round baking dish). Sprinkle with nutmeg or cinnamon. Place cups or baking dish in a 9x13 inch baking pan and pour hot water into pan to a depth of 1 inch.

Bake in a 350 degree oven for 25 to 30 minutes (50 to 60 minutes for 1-quart dish) or until a knife inserted just off center of custard comes out clean. Custard should jiggle slightly in center when gently shaken--it will set up upon cooling. Remove custard from hot water immediately; cool. Makes 5 or 6 servings.

Ingleneuk Teahouse
Proprietor/Head Chef Scott Perrine

CAFE SCAMPI

1/2 oz. Galiano
1/2 oz. dark creme de cacao
1/2 oz. Grand Marnier

Cinnamon stick
Whipped cream
Hot fresh coffee

Put coffee in cup, add Galiano, creme de cacao. Top with whipped cream. Drape Grand Marnier over whipped cream. Put in cinnamon stick and serve.

Scampi
Head Chef/Proprietor Joseph P. Kirkwood

FRESH STRAWBERRIES WITH ZABAJONE

1 lb. fresh strawberries, washed,
    stems removed and cut in
    half

ZABAJONE:

3 egg yolks
2 oz. marsala wine
2 oz. brandy or whiskey

3 tbsp. sugar
1 tsp. water
a Few drops of lemon juice

Arrange the strawberries on serving dish. Place all the zabajone ingredients in a metal bowl over hot water. Mix with a whisk until the mixture thickens, do not cook the egg too quickly. Pour the zabajone over the strawberries and serve immediately.

Scampi
Proprietor/Chef Joseph P. Kirkwood

GLAZED APPLE WITH POPPY SEED PASTA

APPLES:

12 sm. lady apples
2 tbsp. sugar

1/2 tsp. cinnamon
Pinch of nutmeg

PASTA:

1 egg
1 c. all-purpose flour

3 tbsp. powdered sugar
1 tsp. poppy seeds

ICE CREAM:

1 c. vanilla ice cream
5 oz. dark coating chocolate
2 tsp. butter

Heavy cream
Walnuts and raisins to taste

For the apples, peel and core and dust with sugar, cinnamon and nutmeg. Place in a 350 degree oven for 10 minutes. Keep warm.

For pasta, combine egg, flour and sugar and add poppy seeds. Knead to a dough. Allow to rest 3 hours. Cut into fettuccine noodles with a pasta machine. Place noodles in boiling salted water and boil until al dente. Drain and rinse with cold water.

For ice cream, divide in half and place in an ice cream mold to make an apple shape. Freeze and remove. Drip in dark coating chocolate. Let set and score with paring knife to get an apple peel effect.

Heat noodles in butter and some cream and add enough walnuts and raisins to taste. Arrange on plate. Cut apples in halves or wedges and place on plate. Before serving, add ice cream apple to plate. Garnish with pulled sugar flower. Serves 2.

Towne Crier Inn
Chef/Proprietor David Iannucci

PEACHES AND CREAM PIE

BATTER:

3/4 c. flour
1 tsp. baking powder
1/2 tsp. salt

3 oz. pkg. vanilla pudding
1 egg
1/2 c. milk

TOPPING:

1 (15 oz.) can peaches, drained
(save juice)
1 (8 oz.) cream cheese

1/2 c. sugar
3 tbsp. juice from peaches

Combine batter ingredients 2 minutes at medium speed. Put batter in 9-inch cake pan. Put peaches on top. Pour cream on topping. Bake at 350 degrees for 30-35 minutes.

Palumbo's Edgmont Inn
Executive Head Chef Richard Hudson

BREAD AND BUTTER PUDDING

1 qt. milk
4 oz. sugar
Salt to taste
Vanilla to taste

Nutmeg to taste
2 oz. eggs
10 bread slices

Scald milk. Beat together sugar, salt, vanilla, nutmeg, and eggs and add to milk. Remove crust from bread, slice thin, brush with butter and cut each slice in half. Place bread slices in a pudding pan. Sprinkle with a few raisins and pour custard mixture over slices. Place dish on a pan containing water and bake at 400 degrees until firm.

VANILLA SAUCE FOR BREAD PUDDING:

1 pt. light cream	6 egg yolks
1/4 c. vanilla extract	Salt to taste
4 oz. sugar	

Combine the cream, vanilla and 1/2 sugar and heat to boiling. Add egg yolks and remaining sugar cooking over low heat until mixture lightly coats the back of a spoon. Strain the sauce and refrigerate.

Palumbo's Edgmont Inn
Executive Head Chef Richard Hudson

PECAN CARAMEL SAUCE FOR CHOCOLATE BREAD PUDDING

2 c. cane sugar	1/2 c. light Karo syrup
2 c. water	1 pt. heavy cream
1 tsp. lemon juice	1 c. chopped pecans

Mix sugar and water together. Place on stove and bring to boiling. Add lemon juice and Karo syrup. Cook until amber in color. Remove from stove and pour in heavy cream. Finish sauce with nuts. Pour over portions of warmed Chocolate Bread Pudding.

Central Bar and Grille
Chef Hugh Moran

CHOCOLATE BREAD PUDDING

16 c. milk	8 c. sugar (2 c. = 16 oz.)
16 c. heavy cream	90 eggs
2 lb. bittersweet chocolate	8 tbsp. vanilla extract
2 lb. unsweetened chocolate	4 loaves challah bread

Scald the milk and heavy cream. Melt the chocolate in a bowl over hot water. Mix sugar, eggs and vanilla and set aside.

Temper egg mixture with hot milk mixture by pouring a little at a time while whisking until both are combined. Pour through a china cap and add melted chocolate. Whisk together. Pour the mixture over 4 loaves of cubed challah bread and moisten with 3 cups of heavy cream.

Be sure to stir mixture to soak all bread and then let the mix sit for approximately 30 minutes. Pour into 2 hotel pans and cover with foil. Bake at 350 degrees for approximately 45 minutes to 1 hour. Check for doneness before removing from the oven. Should be firm and glossy, not soupy. 48 portions.

Central Bar and Grille
Chef Hugh Moran

EGG CUSTARD

3 eggs
1/3 c. sugar
2 c. milk

1 tsp. vanilla extract
1/4 tsp. ground nutmeg

Preheat oven to 350 degrees. In a bowl, beat all ingredients, except nutmeg until smooth and blended. Pour into 4 individual custard cups. Sprinkle with nutmeg. Put cups into baking pan. Add hot water to pan to 1-inch deep. Bake in oven for 30-35 minutes or until custard is set. Cool baked custard to room temperature, then chill in refrigerator for at least 1 hour before serving. Serves 4.

Pike Family Restaurant
Chef Robert Kellock

MARY'S POACHED PEAR AND CHOCOLATE

1 pear, peeled, cored and halved
1 c. cranberry juice
1/2 c. orange juice
1 tbsp. cornstarch and water,
    combined

1 brick of semi-sweet chocolate
1 tbsp. butter

Place pear halves in 8x8 inch cake pan. Combine cranberry and orange juice, add to pan and cover. Cook until pear is tender. Remove and chill pear. Remove juice from pan and place in saucepot. Heat until boiling, add cornstarch and water mixture. Cook until clear. Chill.

Melt chocolate and butter. Hold until serving time. Arrange pear in fan-like fashion on plate by slicing pear 1/2 inch julienne slices. Top pear with chilled juices (about 3 tablespoons) and drizzle chocolate mixture over pear. Serve.

Tymes Square
Pastry Chef Mary M. Berrie

BANANAS FOSTER

4 tbsp. (1/2 stick) sweet butter
4 tbsp. brown sugar
1/4 tsp. cinnamon
2 tbsp. banana liqueur

3 oz. dark rum
1 1/2 c. French vanilla ice cream
2 ripe bananas, peeled and sliced
   lengthwise

Melt butter in a sauteed pan. Add brown sugar and stir until sugar is melted. Add bananas and saute until tender about 3 minutes on each side. Sprinkle with cinnamon.

Pour banana liqueur and rum over bananas. Shake pan to distribute the liquid and flame. Baste bananas with the flaming sauce until flames die out. Serve immediately over the ice cream. Serves 2.

Cafe Nola
Executive Chef Marco Carrozza
Chef de Cuisine Tom Downing

ESPRESSO TORTE

1 lb. 14 oz. semi-sweet chocolate
1 lb. 14 oz. sweet unsalted butter
1 dozen lg. eggs

1/2 oz. coffee extract
12 oz. granulated sugar
4 oz. strong black coffee

Melt the chocolate and butter on the stove at medium heat. Whisk together the eggs and sugar until combined. When the chocolate mixture is melted, remove from heat. Whisk in the egg and sugar mixture. Add the coffee extract and coffee.

Prepare a 10-inch cake pan. Line the inside with foil (bottom and sides). Make sure there are no tears in the foil. Spray lightly with "Pam." Bake in a water bath for 1 hour at 350 degrees.

Let set overnight in the refrigerator. Flip it onto a plate so it is upside down, then remove the foil (leave upside down). Decorate the top with whipped cream and dust with cocoa powder.

Septembers Place
Pastry Chef Michelle Keller

FROZEN VANILLA HONEY MOUSSE

2/3 c. sugar
1 c. Brie Vermont honey
1 3/4 c. heavy cream, whipped

7 lg. egg yolks
1/4 c. Grand Marnier
1 c. water

In a metal bowl, set over barely simmering water. Melt the sugar and water, stirring until the sugar is dissolved. Cook until it is like a syrup.
Add the syrup to the egg yolks in a bowl. Beat the mixture until it is cool. Stir in honey and Grand Marnier and fold whipped cream in. Pour mousse into champagne glass and freeze. Serves 6.

Septembers Place
Executive Chef John Birmingham

APPLE CRISP IN PHYLLO

6 sheets phyllo dough
2 apples, peeled, cored, and
    sliced
1/4 c. golden raisins

2 oz. brown sugar
2 oz. chopped walnuts
1 oz. honey
2 oz. sweet butter

Lay out 1 sheet dough, brush with butter, top with another sheet, brush with butter. Repeat until all sheets are used. Fold lengthwise in thirds. Arrange sliced apples at one end of dough. Top with sugar and raisins. Fold in a triangular shape, repeating the full length of the sheet. Place on cookie sheet. Brush with honey. Sprinkle with nuts. Bake about 20 minutes at 350 degrees.

Marble's Restaurant & Bar
Proprietor/Head Chef Michel Wakim
Chef Michael Klaumenzer

BASIC CHOUX PASTE (PROFITEROLES)

1 c. milk or water
1/3 stick (1 1/2 oz.) butter

1/8 tsp. salt
1/4 tsp. sugar

Egg wash made with 1/2 egg
    white and milk

1 level c. flour   **4 or 5 lg. eggs**

Bring first 4 ingredients to a boil. Remove from heat. Add flour (sifted if need be) in one motion. Stir to avoid lumps. Return to heat. Collect all together in one ball on medium heat. Cook only 1-2 minutes until dries out and white cake forms on bottom of pan. Transfer to a bowl.

Add eggs, one at a time, incorporating thoroughly (4 or 5 are enough). Preheat oven to 450 degrees. Measure to the size of tablespoon. Lay out on a cookie sheet and bake for 30 minutes until brown and outside is firm.

CHOCOLATE ICING:

3 heaping tbsp. cocoa   **Dash of salt**
1 c. powdered sugar   **1/4 tbsp. vanilla**
1 stick softened butter   **2-3 tbsp. hot milk**

Mix dry ingredients in bowl. Add softened butter and gradually mix to high speed incorporating vanilla and milk to desired consistency. Yield: one (9-inch) cake.

Evviva
Chef Larry E. Langley-Ward

EXTRA RECIPES

MAIN DISHES

SAGE

TEMPTING MAIN DISH IDEAS

When broiling meats or bacon on a rack, place a piece or two of dry bread in the broiler pan to soak up the dripped fat. This not only helps to eliminate smoking of the fat but reduces the chances of the fat catching fire.

Tenderizing Meat - Mechanical methods: Grinding, cubing and pounding meat breaks down the connective tissue and makes meat tender. Marinating: Soaking meat in acid mixtures such as lemon juice or vinegar tenderizes meat and adds flavor. Often herbs and spices are included in commercial marinades. Meat tenderizers: These are derivatives of natural food-tenderizing agents found in some tropical fruits (such as papaya) which soften meat tissue only while meat is cooking.

For juicier burgers, add a stiffly beaten egg white to each pound of hamburger, or make patties with one tablespoon of cottage cheese in the center.

Marbled beef, which has intermingling of fat with lean, indicates tenderness and rich flavor.

Pork chops which are light in color are corn fed.

If you rub the skin of a chicken with mayonnaise before baking, the skin will get crisp and brown.

A half teaspoon of dry mustard added to a flour mix for frying chicken adds great flavor.

The darker the flesh of a fish, the higher it is in calories.

Rule of thumb for cooking fish: Cook 10 minutes for each inch of thickness.

To keep raw fish fresh and odorless, rinse them with fresh lemon juice and water, dry thoroughly, wrap and refrigerate.

For fluffier omelets, add a pinch of cornstarch before beating.

Bacon will lie flat in the pan if you prick it thoroughly with a fork as it fries.

Tenderize tough meat by rubbing both sides with vinegar and olive oil. Let it stand two hours before cooking.

To shape meatballs, use an ice cream scoop to make uniform balls.

Main Dishes

MIDDLE EASTERN STUFFED EGGPLANT

2 lb. eggplant
1 lb. ground beef
2 med. onions, chopped
2 c. vegetable oil
1 tbsp. salt

1 tsp. black pepper
1 c. tomato sauce
2 oz. pine nuts
1 c. water
2 tomatoes, steak sliced

Peel the eggplant in strips. Keep the neck attached. Heat off 3/4 of the oil. Fry the eggplant halfway. After being quartered, transfer the eggplant to a baking pan.

Heat off the rest of the oil and fry the chopped onions until tender, not brown. Add the ground beef, salt and pepper. Stir until the ground beef is cooked. Add the pine nuts. Open the eggplant by knife (not all the way) enough to make a little pocket. Stuff the eggplant with beef mixture. Put a slice of tomato on every eggplant.

Pour the tomato sauce over it and bake for 30 minutes in oven preheated to 350 degrees. Serve the dish with rice.

Aldar
Chef Bryant Edwards

SOFT SHELL CRAB SCAMPI

2 soft shell crabs
3 oz. chopped plum tomatoes
1/2 oz. chopped fresh basil
1 lemon, juiced
1/2 tsp. chopped garlic
1 oz. wild mushrooms, sliced

Pinch of Old Bay seafood
   seasoning
3 oz. clam juice
2 oz. whole button
2 oz. white wine
1 oz. olive oil

Dredge crabs in flour lightly. Saute in olive oil until crisp. Add garlic, lemon and wine, reduce by half volume. Add rest of ingredients. Bring to a boil, lower heat to medium and reduce by 1/3. Can be served with rice or your favorite pasta.

Marble's Restaurant & Bar
Chef Michael Klaumenzer
Proprietor Head Chef Michel Wakim

CHICKEN FLORENTINE

1 (8 oz.) chicken breast, boneless
4 oz. fresh spinach
1 whole roasted red pepper
2 oz. Mozzarella cheese
2 slices Prosciutto

Pinch of dried basil
Pinch of dried oregano
Pinch of dried thyme
2 oz. white wine

Flatten chicken breast with a meat mallet. Layer with spinach, red pepper, prosciutto and Mozzarella cheese. Roll up jelly roll style, use toothpicks to hold together. Place on a baking dish, sprinkle with herbs, salt and pepper. Add wine. Bake until browned nicely, about 30 minutes at 400 degrees. Serve sliced with pan juices. Goes well with orzo noodles.

Marble's Restaurant & Bar
Chef Michael Klaumenzer
Proprietor/Head Chef Michel Wakim

PORK LOIN MEDALLIONS WITH SEA SCALLOP MOUSSE IN A FIG RASPBERRY CHAMBORD LIQUOR SAUCE

BEST PORK DISH IN THE DELAWARE VALLEY

CONTEST

6 (1 oz.) pork loin medallions, pounded
6 oz. fresh sea scallops
2 egg whites
Flour for dredging
2 oz. dried pitted figs

2 tbsp. premium raspberry preserves
4 oz. fresh raspberry
2 oz. Chambord liquor
4 oz. chicken consomme'
Salt and pepper to taste

Dredge pork in seasoned flour. Saute pork medallions in 3 oz. butter until done halfway. Set aside on chafing dish.

Puree scallops in food processor with egg whites, add 1/4 tablespoon salt and 1/2 tablespoon pepper. Pour mousse on pork medallions and set in 375 degree oven for approximately 7 minutes until golden brown.

While the mousse is cooking, dice figs and place in the same pan the pork was sauteed in. When figs start to brown, sprinkle about 3 tablespoons of flour in butter and the figs to form a light roux.

When roux lightens, deglaze pan with Chambord liquor. Add chicken stock, raspberry preserves and fresh raspberries. Let reduce; add salt and pepper to taste.

Arrange finished pork medallions on plate garnished with fresh kiwi slices, kale, and fresh raspberries. Lace over finished sauce evenly. Serves 2.

Rossi's Town Inn
Chef Chris Buonopane

CRAB CAKES WITH PECAN SAUCE

(Award Winning Recipe)

1 lb. jumbo lump crabmeat, picked
1/4 c. scallions or Vidalia onion, finely chopped
3 tbsp. red pepper, finely chopped

2 tbsp. fresh dill, finely chopped
1 tbsp. lemon grass or lemon peel, very finely chopped
1 sm. avocado, chopped (sprinkle with 1/2 tbsp. lemon juice)
6 slices white bread, cubed

Place the above ingredients in bowl being careful not to break lumps up in the crabmeat. In another bowl, mix the following:

2 eggs
1 1/2 tbsp. Dijon or coarse ground mustard
2 tbsp. relish
3 tbsp. balsamic vinegar
2 tbsp. brandy

1 1/2 tsp. Old Bay seasoning
1 1/2 tsp. Worcestershire sauce
Few drops of Tabasco
2 tsp. sweet chili sauce (optional; available at Asian markets)
1/2 c. plus 1 tbsp. mayonnaise

Mix all ingredients except mayonnaise together well. Add mayonnaise; then fold in crab mixture; form into cakes while adding:

About 2/3 c. dry bread crumbs to help hold together
Walnut oil

Pecan halves (optional)
Chopped parsley

Saute crab cakes in walnut oil until golden brown. Transfer to 425 degree oven and bake for 8 to 10 minutes until hot inside.

PECAN SAUCE:

2 c. heavy cream
3 tbsp. lemon juice
1/3 c. plus 1 tbsp. pecans, toasted and ground

2 1/2 tbsp. Frangelica or Hazelnut liquor
Salt and white pepper to taste

Reduce heavy cream and lemon juice by half. Add remaining ingredients.

Rose Tree Inn
Head Chef Joyce Fortunato

WILD MUSHROOM AND GOAT CHEESE QUESADILLAS

1 c. sliced, cleaned leeks
1 1/2 c. domestic mushrooms, washed and sliced
1 1/2 c. shiitake mushrooms, washed and sliced, stems removed and reserved
1 1/2 c. oyster mushrooms, left whole
1 1/2 c. portabello mushrooms, washed and sliced, stems removed and reserved
3-4 tsp. chopped and mixed tarragon, chives, Italian parsley
1/2 lb. goat cheese
Salt and pepper to taste

Saute leeks in extra virgin olive oil. Add mushrooms, sear on a high heat until all the liquid has evaporated. Add herbs, salt and pepper. Lay out mixture on a sheet tray to cool. Mix in goat cheese, taste for seasoning.

12 flour tortillas
Vegetable oil

Spread the mixture onto 6 flour tortillas, top with the remaining tortillas. Heat a saute pan until sizzling. Brush with oil. Cook the quesadilla on both sides until brown.

The Restaurant 210 at the Rittenhouse
Sous Chef Thomas J. Harkins
James Coleman, Executive Chef

SNAPPER IN PARCHMENT

1 lg. sheet of parchment paper
5 oz. snapper filet
3/4 oz. fine julienne of red, yellow, green peppers
1/2 oz. green onion, cut on the bias
Pinch of Chiffonade basil
Pinch of chopped tarragon
1 oz. fish stock
1/2 oz. white wine
Lemon pepper to taste
1/4 c. Spicy Cous Cous

Wash filet and season with lemon pepper. Wash and cut all other ingredients. Arrange peppers attractively on bottom of parchment paper. Add 1/4 cup of Spicy Cous Cous to the center.

Place filet on peppers and top with basil and tarragon. Fold parchment, leaving one end open. At time of cooking of entree, add fish stock and white wine. Bake 12-14 minutes or until puffed and golden.

Tree Tops
Chef De Cuisine Guillermo A. Pernot
James Coleman, Executive Chef

ALL JUMBO LUMP CRAB CAKES

1 lb. jumbo lump crabmeat,
    picked and de-shelled
3 tbsp. mayonnaise
1 tbsp. snipped chives
1 tsp. dry mustard
1 tsp. Dijon mustard

2 tbsp. dry bread crumbs
1 tsp. Old Bay seasoning
Dash of Tabasco
Dash of salt
Dash of black pepper
Juice of 1/2 lemon

Combine all ingredients to blend. Lightly toss over the picked crab in a large bowl. Form into rounds. Freeze to firm them up. Pass through the following breading procedure and saute gently in olive oil or clarified butter until nicely golden on both sides, over low heat. (It might have to be finished in a 350 degree oven to heat completely through.)

BASIC BREADING PROCEDURE:

Flour for dredging
2 eggs
4 oz. milk

Fresh challah or any buttered
    bread crumbs

Beat eggs and milk together. Dust crab cake in flour, dip in egg wash, then coat with buttered bread crumbs.

The Restaurant 210 at the Rittenhouse
Sous Chef Thomas J. Harkins
James Coleman, Executive Chef

WHOLE WHEAT LINGUINE WITH HOUSE SMOKED CHICKEN, ROASTED TOMATOES, SWEET GARLIC AND HERBED TOMATO BOUILLON

1 lb. whole wheat linguine, cooked according to box directions
1 lb. boneless and skinless smoked chicken breast, julienned or diced
1 lb. roasted, skinless and seedless ripe tomatoes, med. diced
4 oz. sweet garlic paste

24 oz. fresh or tinned chicken broth reduced to 16 oz.
2 c. roasted tomato juices, reduced to 1 c.
1/4 c. finely chopped tender herbs, such as chives, tarragon, chervil, basil or lemon thyme
4 oz. butter or virgin olive oil

Combine garlic paste, chicken broth, tomato juice and simmer 5 minutes to blend flavors. Add the diced smoked chicken, diced tomatoes and herbs. Bring to a quick boil, season to taste and whisk in either the butter, olive oil or a combination of the two. Pour immediately over the hot or reheated linguine and serve right away.

The Restaurant 210 at the Rittenhouse
Sous Chef Thomas J. Harkins
James Coleman, Executive Chef

DOC LOBSTER

3 oz. lobster
4 oz. scallops
2 jumbo shrimp
6 oz. broccoli
Juice from whole orange
Pinch of garlic
Pinch of salt and pepper
1 oz. clarified butter

1/2 chicken bouillon cube
1 oz. rice wine
1/2 c. heavy cream
Pinch of dried basil
Pinch of minced shallots
6 oz. cheese tortellini, cooked and hot
3 oz. Romano cheese

Saute seafood in butter, add broccoli when seafood is 3/4 done. Add rice wine, herbs, seasoning, bouillon and orange juice. Finish with heavy cream. Reduce. Add Romano cheese and simmer 2 minutes. Present by placing tortellini in middle of round plate with broccoli placed around edges of plate. Top off with seafood and sauce.

Packy's Pub
Head Chef Matthew Thompson

PACKY'S MARYLAND CRAB CAKES

1 lb. jumbo lump crabmeat, picked
1 egg
1 tsp. parsley
1 tsp. lemon juice
Dash of Tabasco
Dash of Worcestershire

Splash of white wine
1/2 tbsp. Old Bay seasoning
1/4 c. bread crumbs
Pinch of dried mustard
1/4 c. mayonnaise
Oil for frying

Mix all ingredients except crabmeat in a large bowl, adding bread crumbs slowly as last ingredient until a consistent binder (not too wet, not too dry). Fold in crabmeat carefully so as not to break up your lumps. Form into 6 crab cakes, about 1 inch thick. Fry in hot oil until golden brown and serve.

Packy's Pub
General Manager Charlie Mayer

GREEN EGGS AND HAM

2 poached eggs
4 oz. grated Swiss cheese
3 oz. milk
2 oz. chicken stock
1 oz. roux (flour and butter heated until golden brown)
1 tsp. capers

Salt and pepper to taste
1 oz. white wine
4 toast points
1/4 lb. sauteed spinach
1 tsp. clarified butter
4 oz. sliced ham

Poach eggs in pan while building sauce in second pan. Saute capers in butter, add milk, white wine, chicken stock, Swiss cheese, salt and pepper and simmer for 2 minutes. Add roux, spinach and ham. Reduce until sauce thickens. Place eggs on toast points. Top with sauce and serve.

Packy's Pub
General Manager Charlie Mayer

CAJUN PRIMAVERA

1 stalk broccoli flowerets
1 med. carrot, cut in half moon
   thin slices
1 sm. zucchini, cut in half moon
   thin slices
1 sm. squash, cut in half moon
   thin slices
Handful of snow peas

1 c. heavy cream
1 tbsp. Cajun seasoning
4-6 oz. Romano cheese
1 oz. white wine
2 oz. chicken stock
Salt and pepper to taste
6 cheese ravioli, cooked and hot

Parboil all vegetables in advance, then saute them in chicken stock. Add white wine, salt, pepper, Cajun seasoning and cream. Reduce by half. Add cheese, then simmer until sauce thickens. Serve over raviolis.

Packy's Pub
Head Chef Matthew Thompson

PORK TENDERLOIN WITH ONION-APPLE CREAM

3/4 to 1 lb. pork tenderloin
6 tbsp. whipping cream
2 tbsp. cream sherry
1 tsp. Dijon mustard
1/2 tsp. prepared horseradish

2 tbsp. butter or margarine
1 lg. onion, thinly sliced
1 sm. Golden Delicious apple,
   thinly sliced
Salt and pepper

Place pork on a rack in a shallow roasting pan. In a small bowl, stir together whipping cream, sherry, mustard, and horseradish; brush half of mixture over pork. Roast, uncovered, in a 325 degree oven, brushing often with cream mixture, for 45 to 60 minutes or until pork meat in center is no longer pink when slashed.

Melt butter in a wide frying pan over medium heat; add onion and apple and cook, stirring often, until onion is soft, about 20 minutes.

Transfer pork to a platter and keep warm. Pour pan drippings and any remaining cream mixture into onion mixture. Bring to a boil over high heat; season to taste with salt and pepper. Pass sauce at the table. Makes 2 servings.

Ingleneuk Teahouse
Proprietor/Head Chef Scott Perrine

SCALLOPS AND MUSHROOMS AU GRATIN

1 c. regular strength chicken
  broth
1 lb. scallops, cut into bite-size
  pieces
4 tbsp. butter or margarine
1/2 lb. mushrooms, sliced
1 1/2 tsp. lemon juice
1 sm. onion, finely chopped

3 tbsp. all-purpose flour
1/4 c. whipping cream
Dash of nutmeg
1 tbsp. chopped parsley
3/4 c. (3 oz.) shredded Swiss
  cheese
Salt

In a wide frying pan over medium-high heat, bring broth to a boil. Add scallops; cover, reduce heat, and simmer for about 3 minutes or until scallops are barely opaque. With a slotted spoon, lift scallops from pan and set aside. Pour poaching liquid into a measuring cup--you should have 1 cup; if not, boil to reduce or add water to increase to 1 cup.

In same pan over medium-high heat, melt 1 1/2 tablespoons of the butter. Add mushrooms and lemon juice and cook until mushrooms are lightly browned and juices have evaporated; remove mushrooms from pan and reserve.

In same pan, place onion and the remaining 2 1/2 tablespoons butter and cook, stirring, until onion is soft. Stir in flour and cook until bubbly. Remove pan from heat and gradually stir in reserved poaching broth. Return to heat and cook, stirring, until sauce boils and thickens. Stir in reserved mushrooms, cream, and nutmeg. Remove from heat and stir in parsley, 1/4 cup of the cheese, and scallops. Season to taste with salt.

Divide mixture evenly among three 1 1/2 cup ramekins or 6 purchased scallop shells and sprinkle remaining 1/2 cup cheese evenly over mixture in each. If made ahead, cool, cover, and refrigerate until next day.

Bake, uncovered, in a preheated 400 degree oven for 12 to 15 minutes or until hot and bubbly. Makes 6 appetizer servings or 3 main-dish servings.

Ingleneuk Teahouse
Proprietor/Head Chef Scott Perrine

FISH STEAKS WITH ROSEMARY

1 to 1 1/2 lb. halibut, salmon, or
  swordfish steaks, each about
  1 inch thick
Salt and pepper
All-purpose flour

1/3 c. olive oil
1/4 c. white wine vinegar
2 tbsp. water
3 cloves garlic
1/2 tsp. fresh or dry rosemary

Lightly sprinkle fish with salt and pepper. Dust with flour, shaking off excess. Heat oil in a wide frying pan over medium heat until oil ripples when pan is tilted. Add fish, without crowding, and cook, turning once, until fish tests done--takes 4 to 5 minutes on each side. Transfer to a platter, cover loosely, and keep warm.

Add vinegar and water to pan drippings. When sizzling stops, add garlic and rosemary. Boil rapidly, scraping browned particles free from pan, until sauce is reduced by half. Discard garlic. Spoon sauce over fish and serve immediately. Makes 3 or 4 servings.

Ingleneuk Teahouse
Proprietor/Head Chef Scott Perrine

BROWNED PORK CHOPS

4 to 6 shoulder pork chops or steaks, cut 1/2 inch thick
Salt and pepper
2 tbsp. salad oil

2/3 c. dry white wine
About 1/4 c. thinly sliced dill pickle (optional)
Dijon mustard

Sprinkle pork chops lightly with salt and pepper. Heat oil in a wide frying pan over medium-high heat; cook chops, 2 or 3 at a time, turning as needed, until they are browned on both sides and meat near bone is no longer pink when slashed, 5 to 7 minutes on each side. Lift out chops; arrange on a platter and keep warm.

Skim and discard fat; add wine and cook, scraping browned particles free from pan, until reduced to about 1/3 cup. Pour over chops and sprinkle with pickle, if desired. Serve with mustard. Makes 4 to 6 servings.

Ingleneuk Teahouse
Proprietor/Head Chef Scott Perrine

ZITI WITH EGGPLANT

3 tbsp. olive oil
2 garlic cloves, mashed
1 eggplant, peeled and cubed
2 tbsp. minced parsley
1/2 tsp. salt

8 c. chopped, canned plum tomatoes
6 anchovy fillets, chopped
1 lb. ziti

Heat oil, saute garlic in it until brown. Then discard garlic. Add eggplant, parsley, salt, pepper; simmer for 5 minutes, stirring often. Add the tomatoes and cook for 15 minutes. Stir in the anchovies and simmer for another 10 minutes. Cook ziti al dente. Place in a large bowl. Pour in half of the sauce and toss well with spoon. Serve with the remaining sauce spooned on top. 6 servings.

Rosario's
Head Chef Akin Randle

PENNE PASTA WITH BACON AND TOMATO

1/2 lb. smoked bacon, cut into
   1-inch pieces
1 c. chopped onion
2 c. chopped canned tomatoes
1 c. chopped fresh basil

1 lb. cooked penne pasta
1/2 c. heavy cream
Fresh basil for garnish
Freshly grated Parmesan cheese

Place the bacon in a saute pan over low heat and cook until done. Add the onion and cook until onion is soft, about 5 minutes. Puree the tomatoes and chopped basil. Transfer to the bacon and onion mixture and bring to a boil. Reduce the heat to low and simmer 15 minutes. Then add the heavy cream into the sauce, cook for 5 minutes. Then toss with the cooked pasta, garnish with basil and cheese and serve. 4 servings.

Rosario's
Proprietor/Chef Rosario (Russ) Taraschi, Jr.

CHICKEN WITH CAPERS AND OLIVES

4 chicken breasts
Salt and pepper
1 tbsp. olive oil
1/4 c. dry white wine
1/2 c. chopped tomato
Pinch of red pepper seed

1/3 c. Italian olives
1 tbsp. drained capers
1 bay leaf
1/4 c. chicken stock
1/2 c. whipping cream
Chopped parsley

Season the chicken with salt and pepper to taste. In a frying pan, heat the oil. Brown both sides of the chicken. Add the remaining ingredients except the cream and bring to a simmer. Cover and cook for 10 minutes. Remove the chicken and add the cream. Simmer the sauce for 3 minutes to reduce. Adjust salt and pepper to taste. Pour the sauce over the chicken and serve. Garnish with the parsley. Serves 4.

Rosario's
Head Chef Akin Randle

CRANBERRY GLAZED SPARERIBS

3 lb. spareribs
Worcestershire sauce
1 1/2 tsp. salt
3/4 c. jellied cranberry sauce

1 tbsp. grated orange rind
1 tbsp. brown sugar
1 tbsp. lemon juice

Brush both sides of ribs generously with Worcestershire sauce and sprinkle with salt. Place ribs on a rack and bake at 350 degrees for 1 hour.

Meanwhile, in a small saucepan, combine cranberry sauce, orange rind, brown sugar, lemon juice and Worcestershire sauce. Heat to melt and blend. Brush the ribs with glaze on both sides and bake for 20 to 30 minutes. Serve with orange slices and parsley.

Rosario's
Proprietor/Chef Rosario (Russ) Taraschi, Jr.

BROILED MARINATED STEAK

3/4 c. olive oil
1/4 c. wine vinegar
2 tbsp. chopped parsley
1/2 tsp. chopped garlic

1/2 tsp. dried oregano
4 T-bone steaks, 1 inch thick
Salt

In a shallow baking dish, combine the olive oil, vinegar, parsley, garlic, oregano. Lay them in the marinate. Let the steak marinate for 6 hours. Preheat the broiler. Remove the steak. Pat the steak dry and broil it 3 inches from the heat for about 4 minutes on each side or until it is done to your taste, seasoning with salt and serve. Serves 4.

Rosario's
Head Chef Akin Randle

CORNISH HENS WITH ROSEMARY WINE SAUCE

2 Cornish hens
1/2 c. vegetable oil
1 c. dry white wine
1/3 c. white wine vinegar

2 tbsp. soy sauce
1 tsp. dried rosemary
1/4 tsp. dried thyme
4 cloves garlic, minced

Split each hen in half lengthwise. Rinse under cold water and pat dry. Place hens cut side down in a baking dish coated with oil. Combine wine and remaining ingredients. Pour over hens. Bake uncovered at 350 degrees for 1 hour or until done.

Rosario's
Head Chef Akin Randle

FENNEL-GLAZED PORK LOIN

4 lb. pork loin
2 cloves garlic, sliced
8 whole fennel seeds
4 to 6 tbsp. honey

1 tsp. crushed fennel
1/2 c. chicken stock
1/2 c. white wine

Make gashes with a knife along top of loin. Insert garlic slices and fennel seeds into gashes.
Place the loin on a rack and roast at 450 degrees for 30 minutes. Drizzle with 3 tablespoons honey. Drizzle with another 3 tablespoons honey. Sprinkle with the crushed fennel. Pour in stock and wine. Reduce heat to 325 degrees, continue roasting until meat reaches 170 degrees. Place meat on a platter. Skim fat from pan liquid and serve.

Rosario's
Proprietor/Chef Rosario (Russ) Taraschi, Jr.

FETTUCCINE WITH CHICK PEAS AND BASIL

4 tbsp. olive oil
1 garlic clove, crushed
6 tbsp. snipped chives
4 sage leaves, chopped
Salt and ground pepper

2 (14 oz.) cans chick peas,
    drained
1 lb. fettuccine
6 basil sprigs

Heat the olive oil, garlic, chives, sage, salt and pepper with chick peas in large saucepan for about 3 minutes. Add the drained pasta and toss well. Leave the pan over the lowest heat setting while you use scissors to shred the basil sprigs over the pasta, discarding any tough stalk ends. Mix lightly and serve.

Scampi
Owner/Chef Joseph P. Kirkwood
Head Chef Ernest Call

CHICKEN SCALLOPINI ALLA MARSALA

4 1/2 chicken breasts, flattened
   and dredged in 2 tbsp. flour
2 tbsp. olive oil
4 oz. marsala wine
1 c. beef broth

Salt and pepper
2 tbsp. butter
2 green onions, chopped
1 tbsp. flour
Parsley, chopped

Heat the butter and oil. Saute the chicken breasts for 2 minutes on each side. Add the onion and flour, mix well. Cook for few minutes more. Add the rest of the ingredients. Simmer 5 to 6 minutes, stirring frequently. Serve at once.

Scampi
Head Chef Ernest Jackson

LINGUINI WITH BROCCOLI AND SHRIMP SAUCE

8 oz. linguini, cooked accordingly

SAUCE:

4 tbsp. olive oil
1/2 onion, chopped
2 c. shrimp
1 c. strained tomatoes
6 oz. chicken broth
Chopped parsley

2 cloves garlic, minced
1 head fresh broccoli, washed
   and chopped
4 oz. white wine
Salt and pepper
4 tbsp. grated Parmesan

In a large pan, heat the oil. Saute the garlic, onion and broccoli until light brown. Add the rest of the ingredients, except the cheese. Simmer until the broccoli is tender, stirring occasionally. Drain pasta. Toss with sauce and cheese. Serve at once.

Scampi
Head Chef Ernest Jackson

GRILLED VEAL CHOPS, SAGE AND MARSALA SAUCE

4 veal chops, marinated in 3
   tbsp. olive oil

1 tsp. sage
1 tsp. crushed peppercorn

SAUCE:

2 tbsp. butter
4 oz. marsala wine
1 c. chicken broth
1 onion, chopped

1 tbsp. flour
Chopped parsley
Salt and pepper

Heat butter. Saute the onion until golden brown. Stir in flour. Add the marsala wine, broth, salt and pepper, chopped parsley. Heat another fry pan with no oil.
When hot, place veal chops in the pan and cover with a lid. Cook the chops for 4 to 5 minutes on each side, turning once. Add the sauce and simmer for a few minutes. Serve.

Scampi
Proprietor/Chef Joseph P. Kirkwood

FETTUCCINE WITH CHICKEN AND SWEET PEPPERS

3 sweet peppers (red, yellow and
   green)
2 tbsp. olive oil
1 onion, chopped
2 garlic cloves, chopped
1 chicken, boned and cut into sm.
   pieces

2 tbsp. dry white wine
1 tbsp. tomato paste
3 1/2 oz. chicken stock
Salt and pepper
1 lb. fettuccine

Roast peppers over high flame so skins blister and can be easily removed. Cut peppers into strips. Heat the oil and gently brown the chopped onion and garlic. Add the chicken pieces and brown them on all sides. Pour in the wine and the tomato paste diluted with a little chicken stock. Add the peppers and cook slowly to obtain a thick sauce. Add a little more stock if sauce becomes too dry. Season to taste. Cook pasta in boiling salted water, drain and stir in the sauce. Serve at once.

Scampi
Proprietor/Chef Joseph P. Kirkwood

OYSTERS WITH SPINACH AND BRIE CHEESE

6 med. oysters on half shell
8 oz. spinach
2 oz. julienne red onions
1 sm. clove garlic, diced

Salt and pepper to taste
1 tbsp. olive oil
6 slices Brie cheese

GARNISH:

1 red pepper, finely diced   1 yellow pepper, finely diced

Saute spinach, onion, and garlic in olive oil. Season spinach mixture and place on top of oysters. Place sliced Brie cheese on top of spinach mixture and bake at 400 degrees in oven for 5 minutes.

ARRANGEMENT: Arrange baked oysters on plate. Sprinkle red and yellow peppers around plate. Serves 1.

Rose Tree Inn
Chef John Schatz

GOLDEN TROUT WITH HAZELNUTS

2 golden trout filets, cleaned and
    boned
2 oz. hazelnuts, chopped
1 tbsp. butter
1/2 tsp. diced red onion
1/2 tomato, diced

1 oz. white wine
1/2 oz. hazelnut liquor
2 oz. flour
Salt and pepper to taste
1 tbsp. olive oil

Season and flour trout. Sear in olive oil on both sides until lightly browned. Take out of pan. Reserve. Put remaining ingredients in pan and cook until thickened.

ARRANGEMENT: Put trout on plate and spread the sauce across the top. Serves 1.

Rose Tree Inn
Chef John Schatz

WIENER SCHNITZEL

1 (4 oz.) veal tenderloin
1 egg
2 oz. flour

Salt and pepper to taste
3 oz. bread crumbs
1 tbsp. olive oil

GARNISH:

2 lemon wheels
2 anchovies, rolled

6 capers
Sprinkle of parsley

Take veal tenderloin and butterfly. Pound very thin with meat hammer. Season, then flour, then egg. Bread. Saute in olive oil until crispy on both sides. Reserve on double thick towel to absorb grease.

ARRANGEMENT: Place Schnitzel on plate. Place lemon wheels on top with rolled anchovies, capers and parsley on top. Serves 1.

Rose Tree Inn
Chef John Schatz

FILET AND SHRIMP WITH CAPELLINI

3 oz. filet tips
3 shrimp, butterflied
1/2 red onion, julienned
3 shiitake mushrooms, sliced
2 oz. tomatoes, diced

1/2 oz. sun-dried tomatoes
1/4 tsp. fresh garlic
1/4 tsp. fresh ginger
1 oz. sesame oil

SAUCE:

3 tbsp. hoisin sauce
Rice vinegar to taste

1 oz. white wine

PASTA:

Capellini

GARNISH:

1 tsp. black sesame seeds

    Saute all ingredients in sesame oil. Add hoisin, vinegar, and white wine into pan and bring to a boil. Cook pasta in salted water, al dente.
    ARRANGEMENT: Arrange filet and shrimp around the outer edge of plate. Twirl pasta in center of plate. Garnish top of pasta with black sesame seeds. Serves 1.

Rose Tree Inn
Chef John Schatz

LOBSTER AND SHRIMP WITH LINGUINI

1 (6 oz.) lobster tail, cut in half
4 lg. shrimp
2 oz. tomatoes, diced
3 basil leaves, sliced
1/2 tsp. fresh ground garlic
1 tsp. butter

Pinch of finely diced shallots
1 oz. sliced scallions
1 tbsp. olive oil
1 oz. white wine
5 oz. heavy cream

PASTA:

Linguini

GARNISH:

Chopped parsley

    Season lobster and shrimp and saute in olive oil until 3/4 of the way cooked. Deglaze with white wine. Add all remaining ingredients and reduce until thick. Cook pasta in salted water, al dente.

ARRANGEMENT: Place lobster and shrimp on outer edge of the plate. Twirl linguini in center of plate. Sprinkle parsley on top of pasta. Serves 1.

Rose Tree Inn
Chef John Schatz

SOFT SHELL CRABS WITH LEMON CAPER SAUCE

2 soft shell crabs, cleaned
3 oz. white wine
2 oz. flour
1 tbsp. sesame oil
Salt and pepper to taste
1 tsp. Dijon mustard

Lemon to taste
1/2 oz. capers
1 oz. diced tomatoes
1/2 sliced scallions
1 tbsp. butter

GARNISH:

3 half wheel lemon slices

Season soft shells with flour and sear in sesame oil on both sides. Add all remaining ingredients until blended.

ARRANGEMENT: Arrange on plate accordingly and garnish with lemon wheels. Serves 1.

Rose Tree Inn
Chef John Schatz

CHICKEN BREAST WITH OLIVES, ROASTED PEPPERS & FETA CHEESE

1 (8 oz.) chicken breast, cleaned
2 oz. roasted peppers
1/2 oz. diced black olives
2 oz. feta cheese
1 oz. diced tomatoes

Pinch of basil
Salt and pepper to taste
1 tbsp. olive oil
2 oz. flour

GARNISH:

1/2 tsp. parsley

SAUCE:

1 can beef stock
1/2 c. burgundy wine

Juice of 1/2 lemon
1 tbsp. butter

Season chicken, flour, then saute in olive oil on both sides. Then place remaining ingredients on top of chicken. Top with feta cheese and place in 400 degree oven for 5 minutes.
SAUCE: Reduce beef stock, burgundy wine and lemon until thickened. Mix in butter at end. Reserve.
ARRANGEMENT: Place 2 oz. of sauce on plate and place chicken on top. Sprinkle with parsley. Serves 1.

Rose Tree Inn
Chef John Schatz

ROAST FILET TENDERLOIN WITH GRILLED VEGETABLES

1 (10 oz.) filet, cleaned
1 tbsp. olive oil
1 tbsp. sesame oil
Salt and pepper to taste
1 zucchini, angle cut 1/2 inch
   thick

1 tomato, cored and halved
1 bell pepper, cut 3/4 inch slices
1 red onion, 1/2 moon slices

SHALLOT BUTTER:

4 oz. softened butter
1 tbsp. shallots

4 oz. cabernet wine

SAUCE:

1 can beef stock
1/2 c. Madeira wine

Juice of 1/2 lemon
1 tsp. butter

FILET AND VEGETABLES: To season filet, sear on all sides in hot pan with olive oil. Take off heat and reserve filet. Take vegetable medley in bowl. Season and roll in sesame oil. Mark on hot grill or grill pan.

BUTTER: Cook shallots in cabernet wine for 10 minutes. Allow to cool, then mix with softened butter. Reserve.

SAUCE: Reduce beef stock, Madeira wine and lemon juice until thickened. Mix in butter at end. Reserve.

ARRANGEMENT: Take filet on side and slice into 3 pieces. Arrange grilled vegetables on plate. Put 2 oz. of sauce on center of plate for the filet. Place filet on sauce and top with a dollop of the shallot butter. Serves 1.

Rose Tree Inn
Chef John Schatz

BAKED ROUGHY, GENEVA STYLE

1/3 c. olive oil
2 lg. onions, thinly sliced
3 anchovies filets, finely chopped
3 cloves garlic, finely minced
2 lb. ripe tomatoes, cut in 1/4
    inch rounds

Salt and pepper
1 lb. orange roughy
4 oz. sea scallop
4 oz. med. shrimp, peeled and
    diced
2 tbsp. fresh parsley, chopped

Preheat oven to 350 degrees. Heat 1/4 cup oil in large skillet over medium heat. Add onion and cook, stirring until onion begins to brown, 5 to 6 minutes. Add the anchovies and garlic and cook, stirring about 1 minute. Spread half of the onion at the bottom of baking dish. Top the onion with half of the tomatoes, and season lightly with salt and pepper.

Arrange the fish and shellfish over the tomatoes and top with the remaining onions, spreading them evenly over the fish. Top the onions with the remaining tomatoes, season again lightly with salt and pepper and sprinkle with parsley.

Pour the remaining oil over the tomatoes and bake 25 to 30 minutes. Let the dish settle for a few minutes, then with large spoon remove some of the excess oil and watery juices from pan and serve.

Scampi
Head Chef Joseph P. Kirkwood

BONELESS CHICKEN BREAST IN RASPBERRY MARINADE

Marinate 4 boneless chicken breasts in the mixture below for two hours:

1 c. extra virgin olive oil
1/4 c. red wine vinegar
Julienned zest of 1 orange
1 tsp. thyme

1 tsp. sage
1/2 c. finely chopped shallots
1 c. fresh raspberries

Remove from marinate. Roast at 350 degrees for 10 minutes each side or until done. Remove to a serving platter and deglaze the roasting pan with the marinate. Transfer marinate to saucepan and reduce to slightly thicken. Finish sauce with 1 cup fresh orange sections. Serve with the reduced raspberry marinate sauce.

Scampi
Head Chef/Proprietor Joseph P. Kirkwood

VEAL PICCATTA

4 oz. veal medallions, pounded
   thin
Juice of 1/2 lemon
3 oz. whipped butter, lightly
   salted

Black pepper
1 c. flour
2 oz. chicken broth

Preheat saute pan over medium heat. Dredge veal medallions in flour. Melt 1 oz. of butter in pan. When butter starts to brown, add veal. Cook both sides of veal until golden brown. Add lemon juice, chicken broth and pepper. Reduce. Add rest of butter to serve immediately. If sauce breaks, add a little more chicken stock.

Scampi
Head Chef/Proprietor Joseph P. Kirkwood

CHICKEN AND FENNEL RISOTTO

2 1/4 lb. chicken breasts, halved
1 tsp. salt
1/8 tsp. pepper
1/2 tsp. tarragon
2 stalks fresh fennel
6 tbsp. olive oil
2 onions, peeled and diced
1 lg. clove garlic, peeled and
    diced

1 1/4 c. rice
1 1/2 c. chicken bouillon
3 3/4 c. dry white wine
1/2 tsp. salt
1 c. freshly grated Parmesan
    cheese

Rub chicken well with salt, pepper, and tarragon. Cut off some green leaves from fennel; wash and put aside. Trim fennel stalks; quarter heads and wash.

Heat oil in large frying pan with lid. Brown chicken breasts well. Add fennel, onions, and garlic; saute briefly.

Add rice to frying pan and saute, stirring constantly, for 3 or 4 minutes. Pour chicken bouillon and white wine over mixture. Season with salt, cover, and simmer for 20 minutes. Finely chop reserved fennel leaves. Before serving, sprinkle Parmesan cheese and chopped fennel leaves over chicken.

Scampi
Head Chef/Proprietor Joseph P. Kirkwood

GRILLED SIRLOIN WITH ROASTED CORN AND TOMATO SALSA

20 plum tomatoes
10 ears corn
2 c. diced mixed bell pepper (red,
    green, yellow)
1/8 c. garlic, minced
1 c. diced red onion
1/8 c. chopped cilantro

1/8 c. lime juice
2 tbsp. sherry vinegar
1/8 c. olive oil
1/8 c. diced jalapeno
4 (8 oz.) sirloin steaks
Salt and pepper

Remove all but several layers of husk on corn. Place in oven at 375 degrees for 15 minutes. Remove husk and cut corn from cob. Cut tops from tomatoes and place on greased pan and roast in oven until skin is dark and blistered. Let cool and remove skin. Dice tomatoes and place in mixing bowl. Add remaining ingredients except steaks and season with salt and pepper. Chill for 4 hours to overnight.

Season steaks liberally with salt and pepper. Coat lightly with some oil and grill to desired doneness; stir to combine salsa ingredients and spoon liberally over hot steaks.

Bravo Bistro
Sous Chef Stephen Bledsoe

PAN ROASTED VEAL WITH DRIED FRUIT AND FOIE GRAS

2 (3 oz.) mignonettes veal tenderloin
1 c. Swiss chard, blanched in salty water
1 tbsp. shallots, minced
1 tsp. garlic, minced
1 tbsp. sun-dried cherries
1 tbsp. sun-dried cranberries
1 tbsp. dried Russian blueberries

1 tbsp. dried apricots, diced
2 tbsp. raspberry vinegar
1/2 c. port wine
1 c. veal demiglaze
1 tsp. butter
Salt and pepper
3 oz. fresh foie gras, 1/2 inch slice

Saute seasoned tenderloin on both sides for 2 or 3 minutes or until medium rare. Remove veal from pan and add shallots, garlic, sun-dried cherries, sun-dried cranberries, blueberries and apricot and saute for 1 minute.

Deglaze with raspberry vinegar. Add port wine and reduce by half. Add veal demiglaze and reduce on half. Swirl in cold butter and season. Set aside.

In separate pan, saute Swiss chard in teaspoon of butter and season. Set aside.

Saute seasoned foie gras in hot pan quickly on both sides, making sure not to overcook. Set aside.

To assemble on heated plate, place Swiss chard in middle, layer veal on top of Swiss chard and top with foie gras. Carefully spoon sauce around veal and serve with side of roasted garlic whipped potatoes. Serves 1.

Passerelle
Executive Chef Allan J. Vanesko

DUCK CONFIT QUESADILLA

12 (10 inch) flour tortilla
5 duck legs
1 c. sun-dried tomatoes, diced
1/2 c. Poblano peppers, diced
2 jalapeno peppers, diced

1/2 c. fresh cilantro, chopped
1 c. Monterey Jack cheese, grated
5 lb. duck fat
2 c. kosher salt
1 egg, beaten lightly

Trim excess fat off duck legs. Coat legs on both sides with kosher salt and let sit overnight in refrigerator. Rinse off excess salt. Cook duck legs in duck fat at low heat until tender, about 1 hour and 30 minutes. Let cool. Remove meat and dice fine.

Saute diced peppers, sun-dried tomatoes and garlic. Let cool. Mix together with cheese, duck meat and cilantro. Season with salt and pepper.

Lay tortilla flat and place enough duck mixture to cover half the tortilla. Fold over other half and seal with beaten egg. Brown on both sides in hot pan or grill. Serve with tomato salsa, sour cream and guacamole.

Passerelle
Executive Chef Allan J. Vanesko

VEAL JESSICA

1 lb. veal medallions, pounded
1 1/2 oz. smoked salmon, sliced
8 leaves fresh basil, sliced
1 1/4 c. heavy cream
1 tbsp. shallots, minced

2 tbsp. white wine
1 lb. sea scallops
1 tbsp. chopped parsley
2 oz. clarified butter

Dredge veal in flour. In a large skillet, add butter over medium heat. Add veal and brown both sides, then remove from pan. Add shallots, fresh basil and smoked salmon to release flavor. Deglaze with white wine. Add heavy cream and reduce to half. Add scallions and cook until almost done, about 3 minutes. Add veal to reheat. Serve with sauce over veal. Garnish with fresh parsley. Serves 4.

Dugal's Inn
Chef Geoff Young

CRAB DE NANGREDE

1 lb. jumbo lump crabmeat	2 tsp. flour
1 lb. sliced mushrooms	1 1/2 c. dry white wine
1 tsp. minced garlic	Juice of 1 lemon
1 tsp. minced shallots	4 tsp. chopped parsley
1/8 tsp. oregano	1/4 c. whole butter
2 tbsp. olive oil	1 lb. cooked angel hair pasta

In large saute pan over medium heat, add oil and heat. Add flour, garlic, shallots, oregano and mushrooms. Release the flavor of spices, then add white wine and lemon juice. Cook until mushrooms soften. Add crabmeat and whole butter. Divide heated pasta on 4 plates. When butter is melted, spoon over pasta. Top with fresh parsley and serve.

Dugal's Inn
Chef Geoff Young

STUFFED PORK CHOPS WITH MUSHROOM AND SAUSAGE

8 double cut pork chops	3 cloves minced garlic
2 lb. crimini mushrooms, 1/4 inch dice	2-3 c. bread crumbs
1 lb. sweet Italian sausage	2 eggs
1/4 c. onion, diced fine	Juice of 1 lemon
	1/4 tsp. black pepper

Remove sausage from casing and brown in a heavy large skillet over medium heat. Remove sausage from skillet and drain all but 2 oz. of grease from pan. Saute onions in sausage drippings until translucent. Add mushrooms and garlic, then cook until tender. Place sausage back in pan and refrigerate.

When mixture is cooled, add all remaining ingredients except bread crumbs. Add bread crumbs a little at a time until mixture is thickened. Stuff pork chops. In a preheated 350 degree oven, place chops on a buttered pan and lightly salt and pepper tops of pork chops. Bake 45 minutes.

Dugal's Inn
Head Chef Scott Nyman

CRAWFISH ETOUFFEE

2 lb. crawfish tail meat
1 green bell pepper, 1/2 inch dice
1 lg. onion, 1/2 inch dice
6 stalks celery, 1/2 inch dice
1/2 c. olive oil
1/2 c. flour
3 c. fish stock

4 c. cooked white rice
1/4 c. tomato sauce
1 tsp. salt
1/2 tsp. white pepper
3 tsp. garlic
1/2 tsp. cayenne pepper
1 tsp. oregano

Over medium heat in a thick bottom pot, add oil and flour. Stir constantly until roux is browned. Add celery, onions, and spice; saute 5 minutes. Add fish stock and cook 10 minutes. Add bell peppers and tomato sauce. When peppers are tender, add crawfish. Divide rice on 4 plates and spoon etouffee over rice and serve.

Dugal's Inn
Head Chef Scott Nyman

CHICKEN NOLA

8 boneless, skinless and trimmed chickens
8 peeled and deveined 16-20 shrimp
1 c. flour
1/4 lb. sweet butter
1/4 c. chopped shallots
1 bunch chopped fresh basil

1 bunch basil (for garnish)
1 lb. sliced and washed domestic mushrooms
1 pt. heavy cream
2 oz. chicken stock
Salt and pepper to taste
2 oz. brandy

Dredge chicken filet in flour. Set aside. Melt half of the butter in sauteed pan on medium-high flame. Place floured chicken filet in pan and sear on both sides, then place in 350 degree oven for approximately 10 minutes.

In another saute' pan, melt remaining butter and add shrimp, chopped basil, shallots, sliced mushrooms and salt and pepper, while shaking and stirring.

When shrimp start to turn color, pull pan off flame, add brandy, and flame. When flame goes out, add heavy cream and chicken stock. Stir until thick. Remove chicken from oven. Place chicken on 4 serving plates. Place 2 shrimp on each plate and ladle sauce over plates. Garnish with fresh basil and serve. Serves 4.

Cafe Nola
Executive Chef Marco Carrozza
Chef de Cuisine Tom Downing

SHAD STUFFED WITH ROE IN SPINACH SAUCE

2 pairs shad roe
2 tbsp. butter
2 tbsp. chopped scallions
3/4 c. vermouth
Salt and pepper

2 sizes boned shad
1 tsp. cornstarch
1 1/4 c. heavy cream
1/4 c. spinach

Prepare roe first by sauteing them, briefly in butter with scallions or in enameled frying pan, turning them once. Pour the wine over and simmer 10 minutes. Remove the roe, break up with a fork. Salt and pepper liberally and stuff into the cavities of the two-boned sides of shad. Bake in a buttered pan, cover with foil.

While the shad is baking, prepare the sauce by reducing pan juices from the roe. Dissolve the cornstarch in a little of the cream and add along with the rest of the cream to the boiling juice. Add chopped spinach and simmer. After 30 minutes, remove the shad to a platter. Pour the spinach sauce over and serve. Serves 4-6.

Septembers Place
Executive Chef John Birmingham

BREADED VENISON CHOPS

6-8 venison chops, 3/4 inch thick
1/4 c. vegetable oil
2 eggs
2 tbsp. milk

2 c. crushed crackers (onions)
1 finely minced garlic clove
1/4 tsp. fresh basil, minced
Dash of pepper

Heat oil in large skillet at medium heat. Beat eggs, add milk. Dip chops into milk and eggs. Then into crumbs to which you have added the garlic, basil and pepper, making sure they are mixed well. Fry chops until coating is medium brown, and chops medium to medium rare. Serves 4.

Septembers Place
Executive Chef John Birmingham

DEBRA'S ROAST LEG OF LAMB

1 leg of lamb, boned
6 cloves garlic, chopped
1/2 c. chopped mint
1/2 c. chopped cilantro
1 tsp. salt

2 tsp. coarse black pepper
2 tsp. brown sugar
1 tsp. lemon juice
1 c. red wine (the good stuff)
1/2 c. melted butter

Combine the garlic, mint, cilantro, salt, pepper and brown sugar and lemon juice. Spread this mixture over the inner surface of the meat, then roll and tie. Place in a roasting pan and roast at 300 degrees, basting with the wine and melted butter. Cook to 135 to 140 degrees internal (medium).

Septembers Place
Executive Chef John Birmingham

CHICKEN FRANCAISE

(September's Place Specialty)

1 boneless chicken breast	2 tbsp. white wine
1 c. flour	1/4 c. chicken stock
Dash of salt and pepper	1 tsp. cornstarch
Egg batter (see below)	2 tbsp. butter
1/2 lemon	

Combine flour, salt and pepper. Dredge chicken in this mixture. Dip chicken in egg batter, saute chicken in butter until brown, then put in 350 degree oven until done, 10 minutes. Serves 1.

EGG BATTER:

1 egg	1/2 tsp. chopped parsley
1 tsp. garlic, finely chopped	2 tsp. Parmesan cheese
1/2 tsp. Dijon mustard	

SAUCE: In pan, cook lemon, white wine, chicken stock; add cornstarch.

Septembers Place
Executive Chef John Birmingham

CHICKEN DIJONNAISE

4 oz. white wine	12 oz. heavy whipping cream
4 chicken breasts, fat trimmed and cut in half	4 oz. clarified butter
20 med. size scallops	1/2 c. flour
2 oz. Dijon mustard	Salt and pepper to taste

Heat butter in large saucepan over medium heat. Flour chicken and shake off excess and add to pan. Cook chicken on one side, about 1 1/2 minutes. Turn chicken and add scallops, cook additional 2 minutes. Add wine and simmer for 1 1/2 minutes. Add heavy cream and Dijon mustard and cook until sauce reduces to about half. Turn scallops occasionally when reducing sauce. Add salt and pepper to taste. Garnish with fresh parsley and diced fresh tomatoes.

Tymes Square
Executive Chef John Birmingham

VEAL SALIMBOCCO

2 veal medallions, pounded to
    1/4 inch thickness
1 c. flour
Dash of salt and pepper and sage
1 c. chopped spinach

1/4 c. white wine
2 tbsp. butter
1/8 lb. julienned Prosciutto ham
2 thin slices Provolone cheese

Dredge veal in flour, salt and pepper. Cook in pan with melted butter, cook on both sides until golden brown. Remove. Add white wine, sage, and spinach in pan. Cook until spinach is tender, 5 minutes. Add ham and heat. Put veal on metal tray. Top with Provolone cheese and melt under broiler. Remove and arrange on plate. Top with spinach mixture, serve.

Tymes Square
Executive Chef John Birmingham

CHICKEN RADIATORE

8 oz. breast of chicken
2 tbsp. olive oil
1/8 onion, sliced
1/2 pepper, sliced
2-3 mushrooms
1 tbsp. garlic
1 tsp. basil

1 tsp. thyme
1 tbsp. parsley
1/4 head broccoli
Salt and pepper to taste
1/4 c. Chablis
4 oz. Radiatore pasta
Salt and pepper to taste

Saute breast of chicken in olive oil 2-3 minutes per side until golden brown. Add onion, peppers, cook 1 minute. Add broccoli, mushrooms, garlic, thyme, basil, parsley, salt, pepper, and wine. Cover and cook 4 minutes covered. Add cooked Radiatore, salt and pepper. Toss and arrange on a large dinner plate.

O'Flagherty's
Chef Mark Chopko

GRILLED CHICKEN WITH LEEKS AND SMOKED BACON OVER RICE

1 (8 oz.) boneless chicken breast, split, clean, chopped fine
1 tbsp. leeks
1 slice bacon, chopped
1/2 c. shittake mushrooms
1/2 tbsp. pecans, coarse chopped
2 oz. marsala wine
2 oz. port wine
2 tsp. maple syrup
1 tsp. cornstarch
1 tbsp. water
5 oz. rice

Grill chicken until done. Saute bacon on medium-high heat until almost done, about 2 minutes. Add leeks. Cook 30 seconds, add mushrooms and cook 1 minute. Add wine, pecans and maple syrup. Bring to a simmer and add cornstarch and water. Stir until slightly thickened. Place compote on plate next to rice and place grilled chicken partially on top of compote and partially on top of rice. Garnish with light green part of leek sliced thinly into rings.

O'Flagherty's
Chef Mark Chopko

SCALLOPS AND MUSHROOMS OVER SPINACH FETTUCCINI

6 oz. sea scallops
4-6 mushrooms, sliced
2 tbsp. butter, clarified
4 oz. cream cheese
1/3 c. heavy cream
1 tbsp. garlic, chopped
1/2 tsp. shallots, chopped
1/2 tsp. fresh thyme
1 tsp. parsley
Salt and pepper to taste
10 oz. spinach fettuccini

Saute scallops in butter about 2 minutes, then add mushrooms, garlic, and shallots. Cook another 2 minutes, then remove from pan. Add cream and cream cheese. Heat and whisk until smooth. Add parsley, thyme, salt and pepper. Return scallops and mushrooms to pan and pour over hot spinach fettuccini.

O'Flagherty's
Chef Mark Chopko

O'FLAGHERTY'S TORTELLINI

1 (12 oz.) cheese tortellini, precooked
1 (8 oz.) heavy cream
2 tbsp. shelled pistachios, dry roasted and coarsely chopped
5 each asparagus (use 7, if needed), pre-cut in 1-inch sections

3/4 c. wild mushrooms, sliced
1/4 tsp. garlic, chopped
1 tbsp. butter
Pinch of paprika, ground
Salt and pepper to taste

Reduce heavy cream by half. Saute asparagus and mushrooms 2 minutes in separate pan and add to cream along with pistachios, garlic, salt and pepper. Whisk in butter. Put tortellini in boiling water 30 seconds, strain and add sauce. Add a pinch of paprika and place in a large pasta bowl.

O'Flagherty's
Chef Mark Chopko

CHICKEN HUNTER STYLE

4 (8 oz.) chicken breasts, boneless
1/4 c. chopped scallion
1/4 c. onion, diced

1 qt. brown sauce or beef gravy
1/2 c. salad oil
Salt and pepper to taste

Pound breasts and cut into fingers. Saute chicken until lightly brown in oil. Add onions and scallions and cook for 2-3 minutes. Add sauce and simmer over medium heat until chicken is done. Season to taste. Serve over rice or noodles.

Palumbo's Edgmont Inn
Executive Head Chef Richard Hudson

VEAL EDGMONT

1/2 c. salad oil
1 lb. veal cubes
1 lb. cooked sweet sausage, sliced
1 med. onion, sliced

1/2 lb. mushrooms, sliced
1 qt. brown sauce
1 qt. Marinara sauce
Salt and pepper to taste

Saute veal, onions and mushrooms in oil until lightly brown. Add both sauces and sausage, simmer 15-20 minutes until meat is tender. Season to taste.

Palumbo's Edgmont Inn
Executive Head Chef Richard Hudson

ITALIAN STUFFED MEAT LOAF

2 lb. lean ground beef
1/2 c. soft bread crumbs
1 c. onions, finely chopped and
    divided
1 (8 oz.) can tomato sauce
2 eggs, divided
3 tsp. Worcestershire sauce
1 3/4 tsp. salt
1/8 tsp. black pepper

1 tbsp. butter
2 tbsp. green pepper, chopped
1 c. cooked rice
1/2 c. tomato, chopped
1 tbsp. pitted green olives,
    chopped
1/4 tsp. Italian seasoning
1/8 tsp. garlic powder

Combine beef, bread crumbs, spices, 1/2 cup onion, tomato sauce, 1 egg, 1 teaspoon Worcestershire, salt and pepper and mix well. Don't over mix. Place portion into a 9x5x3 inch loaf pan and pat gently to fit bottom and sides of pan, making well in the center.
In a skillet, heat butter and add remaining onion and green pepper. Saute 5 minutes and add chopped tomato and olives. Stir in rice, 1 egg, 2 teaspoons Worcestershire and salt and mix well. Spoon rice mixture into well of meat loaf. Top with remaining meat. Bake in a preheated 350 degree oven for 1 1/2 hours or until done. Let rest in pan 10 minutes before turning out. Yield: 6 servings.

Trieste Restaurant
Head Chef Richard Day

PENNE AND ANCHOVY SAUCE

1 lb. penne
12-14 anchovies
4 c. tomato sauce
3 tbsp. olive oil

5 tbsp. chopped parsley
1/3 c. shredded Parmesan cheese
3 tbsp. butter or margarine
Pepper

Chop anchovies and cook them in olive oil, stirring to a paste. Add tomato sauce to anchovies, with parsley and fresh ground pepper to taste. Bring to a boil and simmer uncovered for 10 minutes. Now, cook the pasta in boiling water for 10 minutes or until tender. Rinse in hot water and drain well. Mix in butter, top with the sauce and sprinkle with parsley and serve with Parmesan cheese.

Trieste Restaurant
Head Chefs John and Anthony Polselli

PASTA PRIMAVERA WITH CLAMS

1 lb. spaghetti
1 1/2 lb. ripe tomatoes, seeded
    and chopped
2 garlic cloves, finely chopped
3 tbsp. coarsely chopped fresh
    basil
1 1/2 tbsp. Italian flatleaf
    parsley, finely chopped

1/4 c. extra virgin olive oil
1/2 tsp. salt
1/4 tsp. freshly ground pepper
1 1/2 dozen little neck clams,
    shucked and coarsely
    chopped

Cook pasta in a large pot of rapidly boiling salted water until tender but still firm, 5 to 8 minutes.

While the pasta is cooking, put all of the remaining ingredients except the clams into food processor and blend to a coarse puree. Drain the pasta and toss it with the chopped clams. Add the pureed sauce, toss well and serve at once. Yield: 6 servings.

Trieste Restaurant
Head Chef Richard Day

CRAB STUFFED CHICKEN

6 (3 oz.) chicken breasts, skinned
   and boned
3 tbsp. low calorie mayonnaise
1/4 tsp. salt
1/8 tsp. white pepper
1/4 tsp. seafood seasoning
1 lb. lump crabmeat
3 slices Swiss cheese, cut in half
3 slices boiled ham, cut in half

2/3 c. flour
1 egg mixed with 1 c. water
1/2 c. bread crumbs mixed with
   1/2 tsp. pepper and 1/2 tsp.
   paprika
1 tbsp. parsley
4 tbsp. oil
Paprika

Preheat oven to 400 degrees. Pound out chicken breasts to flatten to about 1/4 inch thick.

In a small bowl, combine mayonnaise and seasoning. Blend well. Gently stir in crabmeat. Mount about 1/4 to 1/3 cup of crabmeat mixture on one end of chicken breast. Top each with 1/2 slice of cheese and 1/2 slice of ham. Roll up and seal ends. dip each in flour, then egg wash and dip into bread crumb mixture.

Heat 2 tablespoons of oil in a large skillet and brown chicken breast on both sides. Transfer to an oiled (with 2 tablespoons) baking sheet, sprinkle with paprika and bake for 10 minutes. Yields: 6 servings.

Trieste Restaurant
Head Chef Richard Day

CRAB IMPERIAL

1 egg
1/4 c. low calorie mayonnaise
1/4 c. plain, lowfat yogurt
1/2 tbsp. Worcestershire sauce
6-7 drops hot sauce

1/2 tsp. salt
1 lb. backfin crabmeat
1/2 tbsp. Parmesan cheese
Paprika for sprinkling

Preheat oven to 400 degrees. In a medium bowl, mix together egg, mayonnaise, yogurt, sauces and seasonings. Gently fold crabmeat into mixture. Spoon into individual casserole dishes. Sprinkle with cheese, then paprika. Bake for about 15 minutes until hot and bubbly. Yield: 4 servings.

Trieste Restaurant
Head Chef Richard Day

MEATLOAF

35 lb. ground beef, veal and pork
6 c. carrots
8 c. yellow onions
8 celery stalks
2 bushels scallions, finely chopped
9 red peppers
2 bushels parsley
.50 oz. or 2 tbsp. black pepper, ground

5 oz. salt
.75 oz. or 3 tbsp. garlic, raw, chopped
24 c. bread crumbs
40 eggs, whole lightly beaten
5 c. ketchup
6 lb. bacon

Small dice, and pan saute until soft, the carrots, onion, celery, scallion, red peppers and parsley. Season while hot with the cayenne pepper, ground black pepper, salt, and garlic. Mix in the bread crumbs, eggs, and ketchup.

Put mixture into loaf pans lined with bacon, be sure to slap into pans to insure dense meatloaf. Wrap pans to seal in steam and juices and cook for approximately 1 1/2 hours at 375 degrees. For best results, leave pans wrapped to cool. 60 portions.

Central Bar and Grille
Chef Hugh Moran

CHICKEN TERESA

4 (8 oz.) skinless chicken breasts, floured
1 c. sun-dried tomatoes, soaked in hot water for 1 hour
8 pieces artichoke hearts, canned and halved
12 pieces V-15 shrimp, floured
2 oz. garlic

1/4 lb. Prosciutto, sliced and diced
1 c. Marinara
3/4 lb. Brie cheese, cut into strips
2 oz. butter
4 oz. Grand Marnier

In hot skillet, add butter, then add floured chicken and shrimp and lightly brown on each side. Then add garlic, Prosciutto, sun-dried tomatoes, artichoke hearts, Grand Marnier, and Marinara. Then place strips of Brie cheese on each piece of chicken and melt the cheese under the broiler and serve. 4 servings.

Lagoon
Executive Chef Donald Pasquella

CHICKEN ALA ORANGE

4 (8 oz.) skinless chicken breasts,
    floured
1 c. walnuts
1 1/2 c. mandarin oranges

1/2 c. Frangelica
1/2 c. chicken broth
4 oz. coconut
2 oz. butter

In hot skillet, add butter. Place floured chicken in skillet and lightly brown each side. Drain oil. Add walnuts, mandarin oranges, coconut. When coconut starts to brown, add Frangelica and chicken broth. Simmer for 10 minutes. 4 servings.

Lagoon
Executive Chef Donald Pasquella

VEAL AND SCALLOPS PASQUAL

5 (2 oz.) veal medallions, thinly
    pounded
1/2 lb. lg. sea scallops
1/2 c. julienned carrot
1/2 c. julienned celery
4 oz. butter
2 heads broccoli, cut into sm.
    flowerets

1 tsp. curry powder
1/2 c. heavy cream
2 oz. shallots
1/2 c. brandy
1/2 c. diced tomatoes
1/2 tsp. tarragon

In large skillet, add butter and start. Saute the scallops lightly. Add the veal and brown veal lightly. Pull out veal and place on side. Lightly brown scallops. Add carrot, celery, broccoli, curry, tomatoes, tarragon, shallots, brandy. Cream and reduce for 8 minutes and add veal back to dish and serve. 2 servings.

Septembers Place
Executive Chef Donald Pasquella

STUFFED VEAL CHOP

2 (12 oz.) veal chops
1/4 lb. sliced imported
   Provolone
1/4 lb. minced Prosciutto
1 loaf stale Italian bread, cut
   into cubes
1 bag cello spinach, stemmed
   and cleaned

2 oz. ricotta cheese
1 oz. garlic
2 oz. butter
1 oz. rosemary
1/4 c. chicken broth
2 oz. oil
1/4 c. marsala

STUFFING: In skillet, heat up butter. Add cleaned spinach, Prosciutto, garlic, rosemary when spinach is done. Add Provolone cheese, Italian bread, bread, ricotta cheese, chicken broth. Let cook until firm.

Cut pocket in veal chop. Take stuffing and stuff each chop. Place chops in roasted pan. Baste with butter and marsala. Place in oven. Bake for 10 minutes, then turn chops to other side and bake for 10 more minutes. Take out and serve. 2 servings.

Lagoon
Executive Chef Donald Pasquella

BAKED SEA BASS BONA-VISTA

2 (8 oz.) bluebone sea bass fillets
1 bell pepper (red or yellow),
   thinly sliced
1/2 red onion, thinly sliced
1 tomato, thinly sliced
1 oz. garlic

2 oz. fresh chopped basil
2 oz. sliced Mozzarella cheese
2 oz. sliced black olives
1 oz. melted butter
1 oz. virgin olive oil

Preheat oven to 375 degrees. Place sea bass skin side down on hot plate with salt, pepper, butter, and a little water. Place on top of sea bass, pepper, onion, tomato, garlic, basil, black olives, olive oil. Place in oven for 15-20 minutes. When finished, place Mozzarella cheese on top and place back in oven until cheese is melted. 2 servings.

Lagoon
Executive Chef Donald Pasquella

SALMON FILLETS

(WITH WILD MUSHROOM AND ASPARAGUS SAUCE AND ARTICHOKE)

1 med. red onion, finely diced
2 oz. portabello mushrooms
2 oz. morel mushrooms
2 oz. oyster mushrooms
2 oz. kennet square mushrooms
10 spears green asparagus
6 pieces artichoke hearts, canned,
   sliced in half

1/2 c. fish stock
2 (8 oz.) salmon fillets
2 oz. olive oil
2 oz. fresh tarragon sprigs
4 oz. brandy

Place salmon fillets skin side down in oven preheated at 375 degrees. Brush salmon with butter, salt and pepper cooked for approximately 15 to 20 minutes.

While salmon is in oven into small skillet put 2 oz. olive oil, red onion. While getting hot, add mushrooms, tarragon, green asparagus, artichokes, brandy, fish stock. Let reduce until it thickens. Add to salmon when salmon is done and serve.

Lagoon
Executive Chef Donald Pasquella

FILET MIGNON TORNADOE WITH ROASTED PEPPER, GREEN PEPPERCORN AND MUSTARD SAUCE

4 (5 oz.) filets, wrapped in bacon
2 c. roasted peppers
2 tbsp. green peppercorns in
   brine
2 tbsp. Dijon mustard
2 oz. shallots
1 tomato, finely chopped

1/2 c. Madeira
1/2 c. demiglaze
10 pieces sun-dried tomato,
   soaked in hot water for 20
   minutes
2 oz. virgin olive oil

Place 4 (5 oz.) filets in oven preheated at 375 degrees. Cook filets for 12-15 minutes. While cooking filet in hot skillet, add olive oil, roasted peppers, tomatoes, shallots, sun-dried tomatoes, green pepper coins. Simmer for 10 minutes. Add Madeira, demiglaze. Reduce, take filet out of oven. Sauce and serve. 2 servings.

Lagoon
Executive Chef Donald Pasquella

POT ROAST

Pot roast
Goose neck
3 carrots
1 bunch celery

1 onion
1/2 gallon water
2 oz. all season

Chop carrots, celery and onion in large pieces. Put all above ingredients into pot roast pan and cook in oven on 400 degrees for 5 hours. Serves 6 to 8.

Fireside
Head Chef Adolph Funches

GRILLED YELLOW TAIL TUNA WITH PEACH CHUTNEY

4-6 oz. yellow tail tuna steaks
2 oz. black and green
    peppercorns
1 med. white onion, julienne
3 fresh peaches, diced sm.
2 c. port wine
2 oz. cognac

1 c. golden raisins
1 tsp. white pepper
1/4 c. sugar
3 tbsp. wine vinegar
1/2 c. tomato paste
8 oz. butter
1 c. water

Crack peppercorns and lightly tenderize into tuna steak. Cook on covered grill for approximately 10 minutes. While fish is cooking, saute onions in butter in a large saucepan. Add port wine, cognac, water and bring to a boil. Add peaches, raisins, sugar and vinegar. Reduce by half. Add white pepper and tomato paste. Incorporate completely and take off heat. Place finished tuna steaks, peppercorn side up on 4 plates and lace chutney over top. Serves 4.

Rossi's Town Inn
Executive Chef Chris Buonopane

FILET WITH STOUDT

4 (4 oz.) filet mignon medallions
1 lg. Vidalia onion
2 tbsp. crushed garlic
8 oz. butter
3 c. dark beer
1/4 c. honey
1/2 tbsp. salt
1/2 tbsp. black pepper
4 oz. all-purpose flour
2 oz. fresh parsley
4 tomato wedges

In large skillet, saute filet medallions over moderate heat in half the butter to desire temperature. Set aside. In 200 degree oven, in same pan, saute garlic and onions until translucent. Add remaining butter and flour to form roux. When roux starts to bubble, whisk in dark beer and honey. Add salt, pepper and parsley. Reduce for 3 minutes over medium-high heat. Place filet medallions on serving plate (2 each) and lace sauce over top evenly. Garnish with tomato wedges. Serves 4.

Rossi's Town Inn
Executive Chef Chris Buonopane

PAELLA ROSSI

3 c. arborio rice
1/2 tsp. saffron threads
12 white water mussels, debearded and scrubbed
8 little neck clams
4 oz. calimari, cleaned
4 jumbo shrimp
2 (3 oz.) petite lobster tails, halved
2 eggplant, skinned and diced
8 oz. hot Italian sausage, blanched and sliced
1 (32 oz.) can plum tomatoes in puree
3 garlic cloves, minced
1 c. sangria wine
1 sm. onion, julienned
1/4 c. olive oil
Salt and pepper

Cook rice in steamer with saffron until firm. While rice is cooking, saute onions, garlic and sausage in olive oil. In large skillet until garlic browns. Add tomatoes and crush with cooking spoon. Add clams, lobster, eggplant and wine. Cook for 4 minutes over high heat with lid. Remove lid carefully. Add remaining seafood, salt and pepper to taste. Cover and let simmer for 7 minutes. Place finished rice on two large platters or 4 smaller platters and evenly distribute seafood and sauce. Serves 4.

Rossi's Town Inn
Executive Chef Chris Buonopane

IRISH LAMB STEW

10 lb. lamb, half in squares, 1/2 inch cubes
1 1/2 qt. diced potatoes
3 lb. diced onions
3 c. diced carrots
3 c. diced turnips
1 lb. butter
1 lb. flour

Simmer meat in 1 gallon water, remove any scum that forms on top. Continue to simmer for about 1 1/2 hours or until tender. Add vegetables and simmer until tender.

Place butter in heavy pot and add flour to make roux. Do not brown. When meat and vegetables are cooked, add to roux. Mix gently with wooden paddle. Salt and pepper to taste. 25 servings.

Pike Family Restaurant
Chef Robert Kellock

CHICKEN ALA KING

1/2 lb. mushrooms, sliced
2 oz. melted butter
2 oz. flour
2 c. chicken stock
2 c. milk
1/2 c. green pepper
1 c. pimentos, drained
Cooking sherry to taste
2 boiled chickens, diced

Saute mushrooms and pepper in melted butter until soft. Add flour, cook flour for about 10 minutes. Add chicken stock, stir until thickened and smooth. Add milk and mix well. Add drained and diced pimentos. Add sherry and salt to taste. Combine chicken to stock, stirring carefully to prevent breaking.

Pike Family Restaurant
Chef Robert Kellock

CREAM CRAB AU GRATIN

1 lb. lump crabmeat
1 qt. milk
2 oz. butter
1/2 lb. cheddar cheese, grated
2 oz. flour
Salt and pepper to taste
Cooking sherry

In a saucepan, melt butter. Add flour to make roux. Heat milk and add to roux, stirring constantly. Bring to simmer. Remove from heat. Add grated cheese, cooking sherry, salt and pepper to taste, stirring constantly. Mix in crabmeat. Place in casserole and boil until lightly brown, approximately 2 minutes. Can garnish with paprika and/or parsley.

Pike Family Restaurant
Chef Robert Kellock

GRILLED SALISBURY STEAK

2 1/2 lb. ground beef
3 oz. finely chopped onions
3 oz. chopped green peppers

1 egg
1 oz. Worcestershire sauce
Garlic salt and pepper

Mix all ingredients together thoroughly in large bowl. Weigh out into 6-7 oz. portions. Form into oval patty. Grill, broil or bake at 325 degrees to desired doneness. Serves 6.

SERVING SUGGESTIONS: Onion and mushroom gravy, chopped tomato, peppers, onion sauce, top with grilled onions.

Pike Family Restaurant
Chef Robert Kellock

BEEF AND PEPPER STEAK

2 lb. beef round, cut into thin
   slices
1/2 lb. green pepper, cut julienne
1/4 lb. onion, cut julienne
1/4 lb. celery, cut julienne

1 c. water
1 oz. soy sauce
1 oz. A-1 sauce
Cornstarch
Salt and pepper to taste

Place sliced beef and 1 cup water into saucepan. Bring to boil. Add onions and celery. Simmer until tender. Add soy sauce and A-1 sauce. Mix 1 oz. water and 1 oz. cornstarch together. Add to beef in saucepan. Salt and pepper to taste. Bring to boil. Remove from heat. Add green peppers. Cover tightly. Serve over bed of rice.

Pike Family Restaurant
Chef Robert Kellock

CHICKEN DIVAN WITH MUSHROOM SAUCE

5-6 oz. boneless skinless chicken breast
1 bunch broccoli spears
1/2 lb. fresh mushroom, sliced
1 c. milk
2 tbsp. butter
2 tbsp. flour
Parmesan cheese

Pound chicken breast. Place broccoli spears on breast and wrap into bundle. Put chicken bundles into baking pan. Lightly cover with aluminum foil. Bake at 300 degrees for 40 minutes.

MUSHROOM SAUCE:

Saute fresh mushrooms in butter. Add flour to make roux. Heat milk to just before boiling. Add to roux, stirring constantly. Bring to low simmer and remove from heat. Salt and pepper to taste. To serve, pour mushroom sauce over chicken bundle. Serves 5.

Pike Family Restaurant
Chef Robert Kellock

PAN SEARED SWORDFISH WITH FRESH DILL

Tender swordfish steaks pan seared complemented with a heavenly cream sauce with a sweet taste of crabmeat and pungent fresh dill.

2 (7 oz.) pieces of swordfish steak
1/2 c. champagne
1 tbsp. fresh chopped dill
1 tbsp. butter
Juice of 1 lemon
1/4 c. heavy cream
3 oz. jumbo lump crabmeat
1/4 c. corn oil
1 finely chopped shallot

In hot skillet, heat oil; place floured fish in pan and brown on each side for 3 minutes. Discard oil. Add champagne and shallots and reduce until almost dry. Remove fish from pan. Add cream and reduce by half. Swirl in butter, add fresh dill and crabmeat. Salt and pepper to taste. Place fish on plate and finish with sauce.

Bobby's Seafood Restaurant
Executive Chef Bob Donovan

SAUTEED FILET OF GROUPER WITH FRANGELICO CREAM AND TOASTED ALMONDS

A nice white, meaty fish with a sweet taste. The sauce is a rich complement.

2 (7 oz.) grouper filets
1/2 c. Frangelico
1/2 c. sliced, blanched almonds

1/2 c. heavy cream
1 tbsp. chopped, fresh parsley
Oil to cover skillet

In skillet at medium heat, place floured filets, cooking on both sides for about 4 1/2 minutes.

In separate pan over low heat, brown almonds, add Frangelico and heavy cream to reduce. Add fresh parsley. Pour equal amounts over fish on serving plates.

Bobby's Seafood Restaurant
Executive Chef Bob Donovan

SAUTEED POMPANO WITH BLACK PEPPER, CAPER LEMON BUTTER

2 (7 oz.) Pompano filets
1 tbsp. black pepper
1 tbsp. capers
1 peeled and chopped shallot

Juice of 2 lemons
3/4 c. dry white wine
4 tbsp. butter
Olive oil to cover pan

In a saute pan, heat oil over medium flame. Salt, pepper and flour fish; add to pan. Cook on both sides for 5 minutes on each side. Remove fish from pan, place aside.

Using same pan, discard oil, add shallots, capers and deglaze with white wine. Reduce, add butter, stirring constantly, add lemon juice. Pour over fish and serve.

Bobby's Seafood Restaurant
Executive Chef Bob Donovan

CHAR-GRILLED NEW YORK STRIP STEAK WITH ROASTED RED PEPPERS AND BRIE CHEESE

The rich flavor of Brie cheese and the subtle sweetness of the roasted red peppers accents the New York strip nicely. An easy but eloquent dish.

2 (10 oz.) New York strip steaks, trimmed
4 oz. Brie cheese, sliced thin

1 whole roasted red pepper, sliced in strips

Salt and pepper steaks. Grill to preferred temperature. Add strips of roasted red pepper, top with Brie cheese until melted. Serve.

Bobby's Seafood Restaurant
Executive Chef Bob Donovan

CHICKEN SONOMA

8 boneless skinless chicken breasts
8 med. mushrooms
1 yellow (sunshine) pepper
1 red bell pepper
1 green bell pepper
2 oz. Sonoma Brand sun-dried tomatoes
3 oz. virgin olive oil

1 oz. crushed garlic or chopped shallots
1 lb. fresh herb linguini
Salt
Pepper
Hot pepper
Oregano
Ground rosemary

Slice tomatoes and peppers julienne style. Slice mushrooms, cook pasta to al dente. Place olive oil in saute pan with crushed garlic at high flame. Place chicken breasts in pan, cook for 2 minutes, then turn over chicken and add mushrooms, peppers and sun-dried tomatoes. Cook for another 2 minutes and then start to season. Add a pinch of salt--go heavy on granulated garlic and black pepper. Add crushed red pepper lightly with oregano and ground rosemary.

Toss chicken and peppers around the pan and lower the heat and let dish cook until ingredients are fully cooked. Do not over cook--peppers should be soft but still firm. When finished cooking, place linguini on dishes and top with chicken mixture. Serves 4.

Cafe Elana
Head Chef/Proprietor Dominic Di Ventura

SEAFOOD BRIANA

8 oz. sea scallops
8 oz. lg. shrimp, cleaned
1 c. light cream
1 sm. handful sun-dried
   tomatoes
1/4 c. crushed tomatoes

Salt to taste
Pepper to taste
1/2 tsp. Old Bay seasoning
1 tbsp. butter
1 c. heavy cream

Steam scallops and shrimp in large saucepan until slightly firm; drain off excess broth. Add in crushed tomatoes, sun-dried tomatoes and heavy cream. Season with salt and pepper to taste and sprinkle some Old Bay seasoning on top.

Mix over heat until sauce starts to thicken and finish with 1 tablespoon butter with flour and reduce sauce. Best served over angel hair pasta; garnish with chopped scallions and sun-dried tomato bits. Serves 4.

Cafe Elana
Head Chef/Proprietor Dominic Ventura

SEAFOOD ISABELLA

8 oz. sea scallops
8 oz. med. shrimp
4 oz. lump crabmeat
12 asparagus tips, steamed
1 c. chicken stock
Salt and pepper to taste

Crushed red pepper to taste
1 clove garlic, crushed
1 oz. sun-dried tomatoes
1/2 c. white wine
1 tbsp. butter
1 tbsp. flour

Mix together 1 tablespoon butter and 1 tablespoon flour. Saute scallops and shrimp in large pan with olive oil. Add in sun-dried tomatoes and asparagus tips. Toss over heat. Then add in crushed garlic, red pepper, salt and pepper. Cook until tender. Splash with white wine. Lower heat. Pour in chicken stock and simmer. Finish with butter mixture and crabmeat. Serve over angel hair pasta. Serves 4.

Cafe Elana
Head Chef/Proprietor Dominic Ventura

POACHED ROUGHY WITH ORANGE AND FENNEL

1/4 c. orange juice
1/4 c. dry white wine
1 tbsp. white wine vinegar
2 shallots, chopped fine
1/2 tsp. fennel shells
2 strips orange zest, peel off
    skin, make strips with
    vegetable peeler

1/2 c. water
2 fillets orange roughy
1 tbsp. unsalted butter

In skillet, boil orange juice, wine and vinegar with shallots, fennel seed, and orange strips. Add fish.

Shake skillet to keep fish from sticking until most of the liquid is gone. Remove fish. Reduce liquid 1/3 more, whisk in butter. Serve over fish. Serves 2.

Kathryn's Inn
Head Chef Jerry Gonzalez

VEAL WITH TAMARI AND GINGER SAUCE

1 1/2 lb. veal fillet, cut into
    1-inch thick medallions
1 1/4 c. demi-glaze (mixes
    available in supermarkets)
1/3 c. tamari (type of soy sauce)
3/4 c. cashews

1 1/4 c. cherry tomatoes
2 tbsp. julienne of fresh ginger,
    cut into sm. match-like strips
1 1/2 tbsp. garlic, chopped
8 tbsp. cold unsalted butter
3 tbsp. vegetable oil

In a heavy pan, heat 1 1/2 tablespoons of butter, 2 1/2 tablespoons of oil on moderate heat. Add veal and saute. Pat veal dry with flour, salt and pepper. Cook each side for 2 minutes or less. Remove veal, cover, set aside.

Drain oil and butter from skillet. Add demi-glaze and tamari, scraping brown pieces from bottom of skillet. Add cashews, ginger, tomatoes, cook and stir for 1 minute. Add remaining 6 tablespoons of butter, cut into pieces. Heat on low until butter melts, stirring constantly.

In small pan, cook garlic in remaining oil until brown. Drain, pat dry with paper towels. Serve veal topped with sauce and garlic.

Kathryn's Inn
Head Chef Jerry Gonzalez

FLOUNDER STUFFED WITH SUN-DRIED TOMATOES, FETA, SPINACH, AND PINE NUTS

1/2 c. Bermuda onion, diced fine
2 tbsp. olive oil
1 1/2 tsp. minced garlic
1/4 c. pine nuts, toasted lightly
1/2 c. oil-packed sun-dried
    tomatoes, drained and cut
    into thin strips

1 c. feta, crumbled
2 tbsp. grated Romano
1 tsp. fresh marjoram, diced
2 boneless chicken breasts,
    skinned and halved
1 c. tomato sauce
1 c. chopped fresh spinach

Preheat oven to 350 degrees. In a skillet (which can be baked), cook onion with 1 tablespoon oil. Stir until soft. Add garlic. Transfer mix into a bowl, stir in chopped spinach, pine nuts, tomato, cheeses, marjoram, salt and pepper to taste.

With a sharp paring knife, start at thick end of breast, cut a pocket without cutting sides. Fill each piece with equal amounts.

In same skillet, add remaining tablespoon of oil and heat (not too hot, not smoking). Brown chicken on both sides. Transfer to oven. Bake until cooked through, 12 minutes. Serves 2 to 4.

Kathryn's Inn
Head Chef Jerry Gonzalez

PASTA JAMBALAYA

4 boneless chicken breasts, sliced
    1/4 inch strips
8 shrimp, peeled and deveined
8 oz. crawfish tail meat
8 oz. julienne Tasso
8 oz. andouille sausage
1 green bell pepper, diced
1 yellow bell pepper, diced
1 red bell pepper, diced
8 tomato wedges
4 tbsp. Creole seafood seasoning

2 tbsp. ground black pepper
1/4 c. olive oil
1/2 c. bourbon
3 tbsp. chopped garlic
3 tbsp. shallot, chopped
1/4 c. chicken stock
1/2 c. heavy cream
Salt to taste
16 oz. cooked fettuccine
1 bunch chopped parsley
1 bunch chopped scallion

Pour olive oil into large saute pan and place on medium-high heat. Season chicken strips with Creole seafood seasoning and place in pan. Add garlic, shallot, sausage, Tasso, ham, crawfish, and shrimp, saute and stir for 1 minute. Sprinkle the rest of Creole seafood seasoning and pepper over pan. Heat and flame with bourbon. Add chicken stock, heavy cream, and let thicken about 1 minute. Serves 4.

Divide 16 oz. cooked fettuccine equally onto 4 dinner plates. Ladle sauce over plate and be sure to distribute the shrimp, chicken, etc. evenly. Garnish dish with diced peppers, scallion, parsley and tomato wedges and serve.

CREOLE SEAFOOD SEASONING:

1/3 c. salt
1/4 c. granulated garlic
1/4 c. ground black pepper
2 tbsp. cayenne

2 tbsp. thyme
2 tbsp. oregano
1/3 c. paprika
3 tbsp. powdered onion

Combine and mix well.

Cafe Nola
Executive Chef Marco Carrozza
Chef de Cuisine Tom Downing

VEAL NOISETTES WITH CITRUS

SAUCE:

Zest of 1 orange
Zest of 1 lemon
Zest of 1 lime

1 c. water
Veal stock

VEAL:

1 med. zucchini, cut into julienne slices

8 (2 oz.) noisettes of veal

GARNISH:

Reserved fruit of orange, lemon, and lime, cut into perfect segments

Reserved fruit zest

For the sauce, blanch zest in boiling water for 2 minutes. Remove and drain zest. Set aside. Reduce blanching liquid to a third. Add veal stock and reduce by half. Keep sauce warm.

For the veal, heat Teflon pan and sear noisettes for 2 minutes per side. Set aside to keep warm.

Steam zucchini julienne until just tender.

To serve, place a mound of zucchini in the center of plates. Place three medallions on each plate. Ladle sauce over veal and garnish with zest. Garnish plate with reserved fruit segments. Serves 2.

Towne Crier Inn
Chef/Proprietor David Iannucci

SWEETBREADS OF GRAND MARNIER AND BLOOD ORANGES

1/2 lb. veal sweetbreads
1 orange
1 lemon
3 bay leaves

2 c. white wine
2 c. chicken stock
Salt and pepper

In a large saucepan, bring all ingredients to a slow simmer and poach for 20 minutes. Cool. Remove membrane and press sweetbreads between two plates overnight.

SAUCE:

6 oz. Grand Marnier
3 blood oranges, peeled and
    sliced
6 oz. Demiglaze

1/4 c. toasted pine nuts
Fresh chives for garnish
Olive oil
Flour for dredging

Dry sweetbreads and slice in half lengthwise. Season with salt and pepper. Dredge in flour, saute in 1/4 cup olive oil until crisp on both sides. Remove to warm plates.

Deglaze pan with Grand Marnier and add Demiglaze. Reduce to desired consistency. Add pine nuts and chives. Pour over sweetbreads and garnish with blood oranges.

American Bistro
Executive Head Chef James E. Webb

GRILLED BREAST OF CHICKEN WITH RASPBERRY VINAIGRETTE

8 (6 oz.) chicken breasts
1 qt. raspberry vinaigrette
1/2 c. orange juice
1 1/2 c. raspberry vinegar
2 c. salad oil

1/4 c. fresh parsley
1/3 c. fresh thyme
Salt and pepper
2 oz. chopped shallots
1 tbsp. Dijon mustard

In a mixing bowl, whisk together mustard, vinegars and orange juice. When smooth, slowly whisk in oil, then add herbs and salt and pepper to taste.

Marinate chicken in vinaigrette 4 hours. Keep 1 cup of vinaigrette for later. Grill chicken about 3-4 minutes on each side. Serve with reserved vinaigrette or serve on a roll with lettuce, tomato and herb mayonnaise. 8 portions.

Thyme Catering
Christine Amarosa Neugebauer, C.W.C.

SHRIMP AND CRAB, FETTUCCINI ROSA

3 lb. raw shrimp, peeled (16-20 count)
1 lb. crabmeat, pick for shells
1/2 c. olive oil
2 qt. tomato sauce
1 qt. heavy cream
1 bunch fresh basil

1 c. sun-dried tomatoes
1 lg. zucchini, sliced
1/2 c. white wine
1 lb. wild mushrooms
1 lb. white fresh fettuccini
1 lb. green fresh fettuccini

In a large brazier, saute shrimp. Add tomato sauce and white wine; reduce to low simmer. Saute zucchini and mushrooms and add it to tomato sauce. Add crabmeat. Reduce cream by half, add it to tomato sauce. Add fresh basil last. Meanwhile, boil water and cook fettuccini. Serve shrimp and sauce over fettuccini. Serves 8.

Thyme Catering
Christine Amarosa Neugebauer, C.W.C.

GRILLED VENISON TENDERLOIN -

2 lb. venison tenderloin
1/4 c. soy sauce
1/4 c. brown sugar
1/4 c. butter
Shallots

1/2 lb. sliced shittake
   mushrooms
1 c. Bordeux wine
2 c. brown sauce

Combine soy sauce, brown sugar, butter. Bring to boil. Glaze venison with brown sugar. Preheat grill, grill until medium rare. Serve with wild mushroom sauce. Saute shallots and sliced mushrooms. Add wine and reduce. Add brown sauce, season with salt and pepper.

Thyme Catering
Christine Amarosa Neugebauer, C.W.C.

CAJUN PAN FRIED CRAB CAKES

1 1/2 lb. crabmeat
1/2 tsp. dry mustard
1/2 tsp. red pepper flakes
1/2 tbsp. Worcestershire
1/2 tbsp. chopped parsley
1 1/2 tsp. Cajun seasoning
2 eggs

1/2 c. mayonnaise
1/4 c. bread crumbs
4 oz. drawn butter
1 c. heavy cream
1 oz. Bourbon
1 tbsp. tomato sauce or paste

Mix all ingredients except cream, butter, Bourbon, tomato sauce. Form into 4 oz. patties and cook over medium heat in drawn butter until browned on both sides. Remove cakes. Add Bourbon, cream and tomato sauce. Reduce by 1/4. Serve over cakes with side of pasta. Serves 6 (4 oz.) cakes.

The Gas Light
Head Chef Mark Van Horn

PAELLA

16 chicken tenders
6 shrimp
12 clams
1 sm. green pepper, diced
1 sm. red pepper, diced

1 tsp. garlic salt
1/4 c. white wine
1 1/2 c. water
1/4 c. tomato sauce
1 lb. angel hair pasta, al dente

Combine all ingredients in large saucepot and simmer covered until clams open. Serve over pasta. 4 servings.

The Gas Light
Head Chef Mark Van Horn

CHICKEN MARABELLA

4 chicken breasts
4 (3 oz.) lobster tails, shelled
2 oz. sherry

2 c. heavy cream
1 1/2 tbsp. whole butter
4 oz. drawn butter

In large saute pan, over medium heat cook the chicken and lobster. When chicken is thoroughly cooked, add sherry, heavy cream, and whole butter. Reduce to desired consistency. Salt and pepper to taste. 4 servings.

The Gas Light
Head Chef Mark Van Horn

SEAFOOD FORRESTARE

Salt and pepper to taste
12 lg. shrimp, peeled and
   deveined
1 1/2 lb. sea scallops
1/2 lb. crabmeat

4 oz. drawn butter
4 tbsp. whole butter
1 tbsp. chopped parsley
1/2 tsp. chopped garlic

In large saute pan over medium heat in drawn butter, cook shrimp and scallops until 3/4 done. Add crabmeat and garlic. When shrimp and scallops are completely cooked, add remaining ingredients and toss. Serve over toast points. Serves 4.

The Gas Light
Head Chef Mark Van Horn

CHICKEN DE PECHE'

4 chicken breasts
2 oz. peach schnapps
2 c. heavy cream
1/2 tsp. cinnamon

4 cinnamon sticks
4 peach halves
1 1/2 tbsp. whole butter
4 oz. drawn butter

Flour chicken breast. When drawn butter reaches medium-high heat, add chicken. Cook on both sides; when 3/4 done, add peach schnapps, cinnamon, heavy cream, and butter. Reduce to nice consistency. Garnish with cinnamon sticks and peach halves. Serves 4.

The Gas Light
Head Chef Mark Van Horn

GRILLED LAMB CHOP AND FETA SALAD WITH BALSAMIC VINAIGRETTE

VINAIGRETTE:

3 tbsp. coarse ground Dijon
    mustard
1 tsp. minced garlic
1 tsp. minced shallots
1/3 c. balsamic vinegar
2 tsp. capers
2 tbsp. sun-dried tomatoes, diced

1 tbsp. sugar
2 tbsp. julienned fresh basil
2 tbsp. chopped fresh parsley
2 tbsp. chopped fresh chives
1 tsp. cracked black pepper
1 c. olive oil
Salt and pepper to taste

In large bowl, combine all ingredients except oil. Slowly whisk in oil. Season to taste.

TO ASSEMBLE SALAD:

6 heads mixed baby lettuce
1 bunch arugula
1 head radicchio
Enoki mushrooms
9 oz. feta cheese
1/2 c. sun-dried julienned
    tomatoes

Julienned red bell pepper
12 French cut lollipop lamb
    chops
Olive oil
Salt and pepper to taste

Arrange lettuces on four plates. Brush chops with oil and season. Grill to medium rare, about 3 minutes per side. Dress salad with 3 oz. vinaigrette; top with 2 oz. feta and lamb chops. Garnish with sun-dried tomatoes, red bell peppers and Enoki mushrooms.

American Bistro
Executive Head Chef James E. Webb

BLACKENED DUCK BREAST ASPARAGUS SALAD WITH RASPBERRY VINAIGRETTE

RASPBERRY VINAIGRETTE:

1 sm. red onion
1/2 c. raspberry preserves, strained
1/2 c. port wine
3/4 c. raspberry vinegar
3 c. blended oil
3 tbsp. fresh parsley, chopped
3 tbsp. fresh scallions, chopped
3 tbsp. fresh basil, chopped

3 tbsp. fresh chives, chopped
1 tbsp. cracked black pepper
1 tbsp. pink peppercorns, available in specialty food stores
2 tbsp. pine nuts
Salt and pepper to taste
1/2 pt. fresh raspberries

SALAD:

3 whole duck breasts
3 lb. stalk asparagus
1 head radicchio, washed

1 bunch arugula, washed
Hard-boiled egg wedges and cornichon for garnish

BLACKENING MIXTURE:

1 part paprika
1 part cayenne pepper
1 part celery salt
1 part onion powder
1 part garlic powder

1 part black pepper
1 part oregano
1 part thyme
1 part crushed pepper
1 part Old Bay seasoning

VINAIGRETTE: In a food processor, process onion until minced fine. In large bowl, whisk together onion, preserves, wine and vinegar and slowly whisk in oil. Stir in remaining ingredients. Keep in refrigerator several hours before serving.

SALAD: Remove duck breast from skin; each whole breast will yield 2 portions. Cut bottom off asparagus. Blanch in boiling water until al dente. Refresh in ice water. Heat large skillet. Add oil, season, duck breasts with salt and pepper. Coat with blackened mix. Blacken until medium rare.

On 6 plates, arrange arugula, shredded radicchio and asparagus stalks. Dress with raspberry vinaigrette. Slice duck breasts on bias and fan across salad. Garnish with egg wedge, cornichons, parsley, pink peppercorn and fresh raspberries. Serves 6.

American Bistro
Executive Head Chef James E. Webb

POACHED SALMON SALAD WITH POACHED PEAR VINAIGRETTE

POACHED PEARS:

8 pears, peeled and cored
2 c. port wine
2 c. Burgundy
1/2 c. sugar
1 vanilla bean, split lengthwise

Combine all ingredients in a large saucepan. Poach until pears reach desired tenderness, approximately 1 hour. Remove from heat and allow to cool. Reserve liquid.

VINAIGRETTE:

4 pureed, poached pears
1 sm. red onion, diced
2 c. blended oil
1/3 c. red wine vinegar
1/3 c. reserved poached liquid
3 tbsp. chopped fresh parsley
3 tbsp. chopped fresh chives
1 tbsp. chopped fresh mint
1 tbsp. cracked black peppercorn
1 tbsp. pink peppercorn
   (available in specialty food
   stores)
1 tbsp. toasted pine nuts
Salt and pepper to taste

In a large bowl, combine all ingredients except oil. Slowly whisk in oil. Season to taste.

TO ASSEMBLE SALAD:

4 (5 oz.) filets Norwegian salad
1/2 c. white wine
2 c. water
Salt and pepper
Juice of 1 lg. lemon

In a shallow saucepan, bring water, wine, lemon juice and salt and pepper to simmer.
Poach salmon until firm to the touch, about 4 minutes. Remove with slotted spoon.

6 heads mixed baby lettuce
1 bunch watercress
1 head Belgian endive

1 head radicchio
1 yellow pepper, julienned
1 bag Enoki mushrooms

Arrange lettuce on 4 plates. Slice remaining poached pears to fan out and place on plates. Dress with 3 oz. of vinaigrette. Place poached salmon on top. Garnish with yellow pepper, Enoki mushrooms and fresh ground black pepper.

American Bistro
Executive Head Chef James E. Webb

SALMON CRAB CAKES

1 lb. Atlantic salmon filet
1 lb. jumbo lump crabmeat
1 red bell pepper, diced
1/2 white onion, diced
2 sprigs parsley, diced
2 sprigs dill, diced

2 tbsp. whole grain mustard
1/3 c. mayonnaise
1 tsp. Old Bay seasoning
1 lemon
Salt and pepper
Bread crumbs

Poach salmon until almost done, then chill. Flake salmon into pieces about the same size as the crabmeat. Add the bell pepper, onion, dill, parsley, mustard and Old Bay seasoning to the crab and salmon.
Squeeze the lemon into the mixture. Add the mayonnaise and mix. Add enough bread crumbs to combine. Season to taste. Form 4 cakes. Dust the outside with bread crumbs. Saute until golden brown. Makes 4 cakes.

American Bistro
Executive Head Chef James E. Webb

BLACK ANGUS SIRLOIN STEAK WITH MUSHROOM DUXELLE AND BRIE CHEESE

4 (12 oz.) Black Angus sirloin
    steaks, trimmed of excess fat

1/2 c. Demiglaze or brown gravy
1/2 lb. Brie cheese

MUSHROOM DUXELLE:

1/2 c. sliced Kenneth Square mushrooms
1/2 c. shittake mushrooms
1/2 c. sliced Portabello mushrooms
1/2 c. rehydrated sun-dried tomatoes

1/2 c. heavy cream
1 tsp. fresh rosemary, diced
2 sprigs fresh sage, diced
1 bay leaf
Salt and pepper
1 sm. red onion, diced
2 cloves fresh garlic, diced

In a large saucepan, sweat mushrooms, onion, garlic, dried tomatoes and bay leaf. Add sage, rosemary and cream. Reduce until cream is reduced by half. Salt and pepper to taste. Chop in food processor until mixture is coarse.

Grill steaks to desired doneness. Slice on bias. Arrange on baking tray. Top with Duxelle and sliced Brie. Melt under broiler. Sauce 4 plates with Demiglaze. Arrange steaks and serve. Serves 4.

American Bistro
Executive Head Chef James E. Webb

GRILLED WHOLE STRIPED BASS WITH JUMBO LUMP CRABMEAT AND FRESH HERBS

4 (1 1/2 lb.) striped bass, scaled and cleaned
1 lb. jumbo lump crabmeat, picked
1 red onion
2 tomatoes, skinned and diced
1/4 c. basil, sliced

3 cloves fresh garlic, diced
1 (4 oz.) jar capers, drained
1/4 c. balsamic vinegar
3/4 c. white wine
1/4 c. extra virgin olive oil
Salt and pepper
3 lemons, sliced in half

Season striped bass with 1 lemon, garlic, salt and pepper. Rub them with olive oil (inside and out). Grill the striped bass on both sides until half done.

Put fish in large baking pan. Add wine, vinegar, olive oil, garlic, sliced lemons and capers. Bake at 400 degrees until done. (To test fish, use a fork by the gill. It should be white all the way through.)

Take remaining liquid out of baking pan. Put it into a saucepan. Bring the liquid up to a boil. Reduce until desired amount. Add crabmeat, tomatoes and basil. Season to taste.

Put the fish onto plates. Divide the crabmeat and sauce onto the plates and into four. Serves 4.

American Bistro
Executive Head Chef James E. Webb

SHRIMP AND SCALLOPS ROSSI

8 oz. shrimp
8 oz. scallops
2 oz. white wine
1 oz. fresh garlic
2 oz. margarine

2 oz. fresh parsley
1 med. tomato, diced
1 oz. flour
6 oz. chicken broth

Put skillet on high heat for 30 seconds. Add margarine, dust shrimp and scallops with flour, add to skillet. Saute for 20 seconds on each side. Add flour, stir well and add wine. Add chicken broth, add garlic, stir well again. Add parsley, add tomatoes, stir well and serve.

Riddle Ale House
Chef Juan Llamuca

CHICKEN EL PASO

1 boneless chicken breast
2 oz. cheddar cheese
1 oz. green pepper, tomato, and
   onion, julienne cut

Pinch of oregano
Black pepper
1 clove fresh garlic
1 oz. black olives

Pound chicken breast. Add cheese. Saute vegetables and spices briskly in light oil. Stuff chicken. Bake at 375 degrees for 10-15 minutes.

Riddle Ale House
Chef Juan Llamuca

SCALLOPINI OF VEAL MARSALA

1 1/2 lb. veal leg, boned
Salt and pepper to taste
Flour for dredging
3 oz. butter

4 oz. Marsala wine
Lemon juice from 1/2 lemon
4 oz. brown sauce
2 tbsp. parsley, chopped

Slice veal very thin into 12 (2 oz.) pieces and pound to flatten. To cook, season with salt and pepper and dredge in flour. Melt butter in large skillet. When hot, place veal cutlets in skillet and brown. Remove to serving dish.

Deglaze pan with Marsala wine and lemon juice. Cook 1 minute, scraping bottom and sides. Add brown sauce to pan. Bring to a boil, pour sauce over meat. Garnish with parsley.

Seven Stars Inn
Head Chef Michael Walters

SHRIMP CALIXO

6 jumbo shrimp
1 oz. flour
1 oz. crushed garlic
1 oz. fresh parsley
2 oz. diced onions
2 oz. sherry wine

Dash of black pepper
Dash of cumin
Dash of thyme
2 oz. margarine, clarified
4 oz. chicken broth

Butterfly shrimp, dust in flour, saute in butter on both sides until golden brown. Add flour and wine, add all spices and chicken broth. Stir well and serve.

Riddle Ale House
Chef Juan Llamuca

PORK AND SPICY APPLES

6 oz. boneless pork
1/2 green pepper
1/2 onion
3 cloves garlic
Dash of black pepper

Dash of cinnamon
Dash of chicken base
Dash of paprika
2 oz. clarified butter
1 whole peeled apple

Blend all ingredients except for the butter, cinnamon, apple and paprika. Butterfly and pound pork and baste with blended ingredients on both sides. Stuff with apples, cinnamon and roll. Pour butter on top of pork. Sprinkle with paprika. Bake at 375 degrees for 15 minutes.

Riddle Ale House
Chef Juan Llamuca

BLACK DIAMOND STRIP

12 oz. strip steak

MARINADE:

1/2 c. oil
2 tbsp. soy sauce
2 oz. vinegar
1 tbsp. crushed garlic

4 oz. crushed onions
2 oz. black pepper
1 oz. mustard

Blend all ingredients in blender. Marinate steak overnight. Cook as desired.

Riddle Ale House
Chef Juan Llamuca

BAYOU COMBO

4 oz. swordfish
4 oz. chicken breast
4 oz. pork loin
1 tsp. cumin
1 oz. white wine
Dash of Tabasco sauce
1 tbsp. mustard

1 oz. flour
1/2 tomato
1/2 onion, sliced (med. size)
1 tsp. black pepper
1 tsp. garlic, crushed
1 tsp. chicken base
1 1/2 c. water

Pound chicken and pork. Dust with flour. Saute on both sides on high temperature. Add swordfish, add flour, spices and water. Remove from flame. Saute onions and tomatoes. Put on top when served.

Riddle Ale House
Chef Juan Llamuca

CHICKEN ROCKEFELLER

1 boneless chicken breast
2 oz. sliced onions
4 oz. fresh spinach
2 cloves garlic
Dash of black pepper

Dash of oregano
1 oz. white wine
1 oz. flour
2 oz. clarified butter
2 oz. chicken broth

Pound chicken breast, dust in flour. Saute in skillet on high flame. Add onions, spinach, spices and wine and broth. Stir well and serve.

Riddle Ale House
Chef Juan Llamuca

BAKED STUFFED SPARERIBS

Milk to moisten
1 1/2 qt. bread crumbs
6 onions, sliced fine
6 oz. shortening
1 tbsp. celery salt
1 1/2 tsp. sage

1 1/2 tsp. salt
1 1/2 tsp. white pepper
1 1/2 tsp. marjoram
Whole egg, beaten
9 lb. fresh spareribs, trimmed

Pour milk over bread crumbs and let soak. Saute onions in shortening until tender. Mix onions, celery salt, sage, salt, pepper, marjoram and moistened crumbs together and add eggs. Mix well.

Crack spareribs across the middle and place the stuffing on one half, then fold over and tie together. Barely cover bottom of roasting pan with water and place the ribs on a rack in the pan. Roast at 375 degrees, turning on both sides until the ribs are brown and crisp on both sides. Yield: 12 portions.

Seven Stars Inn
Head Chef Michael Walters

FROG LEGS PROVENCALE

2 pair fresh frog legs
Milk as needed
Flour as needed
4 oz. olive oil
Salt to taste
Pepper to taste

1 oz. butter
1 tbsp. lemon juice
1 tsp. parsley, chopped
1/2 tsp. garlic clove, finely
    chopped

Dip frog legs in milk, roll in flour. Heat the olive oil in a frying pan to the smoking point. Add the frog legs and fry until golden brown on one side, turn and brown the other side. Remove from pan and place on serving dish. Season with salt and pepper.

Brown the butter in a frying pan. Add lemon juice, parsley and garlic. Blend well. Pour over frog legs. Serve very hot.

Seven Stars Inn
Head Chef Michael Walters

CHICKEN CHASSEUR

5 chickens, disjointed (2 1/2 to 3 lb. each)
2 tbsp. salt
1/2 tsp. pepper
8 oz. salad oil
2 oz. shallots

2 garlic cloves, chopped
1 lb. mushrooms, sliced
8 oz. white wine
1 qt. tomatoes, canned
8 oz. Demiglaze
2 oz. fines herbs

Clean and disjoint chicken. Season chicken with salt and pepper. Heat oil in large saute pan. Add chicken pieces and brown carefully on all sides.

To prepare sauce: Remove all but 1/2 cup of the oil in saute pan. Add chopped shallots. Simmer until tender. Add garlic and mushrooms and saute. Add white wine. Add tomatoes, add Demiglaze. Bring to a boil. Season. Reduce to simmering. Add the chicken, cover and continue to cook for 1/2 hour or until tender. Makes 10 portions.

Seven Stars Inn
Head Chef Michael Walters

POULET A LA KIEV

4 chicken breasts
1/8 lb. sweet butter
1 clove garlic, minced
2 tsp. chives
Salt and pepper to taste

2 3/8 oz. flour
1 egg, beaten
2 oz. white bread crumbs
Watercress for garnish

Skin chicken and remove breast bones. Cut off wing tips, leaving small wing bones attached to the meat as a handle. Place each chicken breast butterflied between 2 sheets of wax paper, skin side down. Beat gently with wooden mallet, starting in the center until 1/8 inch thick. Remove the paper.

In the middle of each breast, place a small finger of firm cold butter, a bit of garlic, 1/2 teaspoon chopped chives, salt and pepper. Roll up and tuck each end. Dust lightly with flour, brush with beaten egg, roll in bread crumbs. Pan fry until golden brown and breast is cooked. Serve on hot platter with watercress as a garnish.

Seven Stars Inn
Head Chef Michael Walters

CRAB CAKES

1 can lump crabmeat
1 egg
5 slices white bread without
   crust
1 tsp. Worcestershire

1 tsp. dry mustard
2 tsp. all season
2 oz. bread crumbs
4 oz. mayonnaise

Mix all ingredients together. Take approximately 2 1/2 oz. portions and shape into cake form. Bread cakes in bread crumbs. Bake in preheated oven at 350 degrees for approximately 10 minutes on each side. (Total 20 minutes) or fry in skillet until golden brown. Serves 4 to 6.

Fireside
Head Chef Adolph Funches

CHICKEN FLORENTINE

1 lb. cooked spinach
8 oz. cooked white rice
1 tsp. granulated garlic
1/2 c. Parmesan cheese

2 tsp. chicken stock
Pinch of white pepper
6 chicken breasts, boneless

Mix all above ingredients together in bowl. Cut pocket in chicken breasts. Stuff with mixture and bake in preheated oven at 350 degrees for 60 minutes. Serves 6.

Fireside
Head Chef Adolph Funches

CHICKEN POT PIE

1 (5 lb.) chicken
3 onions
8 carrots

1 lb. frozen sweet peas
6 oz. chicken stock

Cook carrots in boiling water until tender. Add onions, peas, chicken, cut into pieces, and chicken stock. Cook for 5 minutes. Add flour and water, mix to thicken.

CRUST:

2 c. flour
1 tsp. salt
1/3 c. Crisco shortening

3/4 c. milk
1 tbsp. baking powder

Mix flour, baking powder and salt. Mix in Crisco with fork. Add milk to moisten. Sprinkle flour on cutting board. Roll dough. Take rolling pin and flatten dough. Line pie dish with dough. Pour in mixture and cover top with dough. Makes 2 pies.

Fireside
Head Chef Adolph Funches

SAUTEED SCALLOPS AND BROCCOLI IN WHITE SAUCE

1/2 garlic clove, diced fine
1 carrot, shredded
1 1/2 lb. scallops
1 lb. broccoli, cooked

3 oz. clam base
1 qt. half & half
1 lb. fettuccini
1/4 lb. grated Parmesan cheese

Saute scallops and garlic in 1 oz. oil until half done. Add half & half, broccoli and clam base. Cook until done. Add grated Parmesan cheese. Pour mixture over cooked fettuccini. Serves 6 to 8.

Fireside
Head Chef Adolph Funches

PINEAPPLE CHICKEN BREAST

1 qt. pineapple juice
2 oz. honey
1/2 c. white sugar

5 oz. skinless, boneless chicken breast

Bring pineapple juice, honey and sugar to a boil. Thicken with water and flour mix. Cook chicken on grill until done. Dip in sauce. Serves 5.

Fireside
Head Chef Adolph Funches

CHICKEN AND DUMPLINGS

1 cooked chicken, cut in portions
3 stalks celery
2 carrots
1/2 onion
1 gallon water
1 c. flour

2 tsp. double acting baking
  powder
1/2 tsp. salt
1 egg
1/2 gallon chicken stock

Simmer chicken, celery, carrots and onion in water. Mix flour, baking powder and salt. Break egg into measuring cup until half full. Drop dumpling batter from a spoon (first dip spoon in stock, then in water). Fill spoon with batter and drop into stock. Continue until dumplings are barely touching. Cover and simmer for 10 minutes. Serve at once. Serves 4 to 6.

Fireside
Head Chef Adolph Funches

CHICKEN, BROCCOLI AND TOMATO OVER CAPPELLINI

4 (8 oz.) chicken breasts
2 c. cooked fresh broccoli florets
2 lg. tomatoes, med. diced

1/2 c. minced garlic
Salt and pepper to taste
1/2 c. salad oil

Pound breasts and cut into pieces. Saute chicken in oil until lightly browned. Add garlic, tomatoes, and broccoli and simmer until chicken is cooked. Season with salt and pepper. Serve over a nest of angel hair pasta. Serves 4.

Palumbo's Edgmont Inn
Executive Chef Richard Hudson

EXTRA RECIPES

SOUPS AND SALADS

ROSEMARY

SUPER SOUPS
& SCRUMPTIOUS SALADS

For soup and stew that is too salty, add a raw potato and discard after cooking. The potato absorbs the salt.

Did you know? Cooking in cast iron definitely boosts iron intake. Soup simmered for a few hours in an iron pot has almost thirty times more iron than soup cooked in another pan.

Thickeners for soups can be either flour or cornstarch. It is a good idea to add the thickener with the pan off the heat to avoid the danger of lumping. Flour is good for soups to be served hot. Cornstarch is better for cold soups.

Most important of all, remember that hot soups should be served HOT and cold soups COLD - none benefit from being served lukewarm.

If delayed in tossing salads, greens will stay fresh under a drape of paper towels wrung out of ice water.

Always shake on oil and vinegar dressing just before using.

When unmolding a salad, always sprinkle a few drops of water on the serving plate. It will be easy to move the salad around to position it correctly.

For a stay put garnish in a molded salad, arrange design, pour over thin layer of partially set gelatin. Chill.

To test freshness of dried herbs, rub them between your hands. Oil of your hand extracts the essence of the herb. If there is no smell, they are no good.

Season with seeds to add flavors:
Caraway: Tangy and slightly sweet
Cardomon: Spicy
Celery: Strong, use sparingly
Cumin: Slightly bitter
Dill: Pungent and strong in flavor
Fennel: Licorice flavor
Mustard: Dry mustard is a mixture of ground seeds of several mustard varieties.
Sesame: Sweet, nutty flavor

For crunchy cole slaw, cut cabbage in half and soak in salted water for an hour. Drain well, then proceed with recipe.

Add a small amount of beet vinegar to mayonnaise to give it a pretty color for salads.

CREAMY MUSHROOM SOUP

1/2 c. butter, divided
2 onions, chopped
2 green peppers, chopped
2 carrots, grated
2 cloves garlic, minced
1 tbsp. sweet Hungarian paprika
1 1/2 lb. mushrooms, sliced
1/2 lb. mushrooms, unsliced
1/2 tsp. basil

5 c. chicken broth
Salt and pepper to taste
1 c. sour cream
2 tbsp. chopped fresh dill
1 tbsp. butter, melted
2 tbsp. flour
Fresh parsley and dill for
  garnish

Saute onions, peppers, carrots, in butter for 5 minutes. Garlic last. Add paprika and saute 3 minutes more. Add more butter as needed. Put mixture into pot. Saute mushrooms in butter in small batches 3-5 minutes, add to vegetables. Add basil and chicken broth; salt and pepper to taste. Simmer slowly 1/2 hour.

Dip out 1 cup of broth; mix with sour cream, stirring until smooth. Stir into pot; add chopped dill. Blend butter and flour; thicken soup with blended mixture. Simmer 10 minutes. Garnish with fresh dill and parsley. Yield: 6-8 servings.

Packy's Pub
General Manager/Chef Charlie Mayer

PACKY'S SEAFOOD CHOWDER

1 onion, med. dice
4 sticks celery, med. dice
2 carrots
1 lb. bacon
1 c. flour
1/2 gallon fish stock
1 lb. potatoes
1/2 tsp. basil
1/2 tsp. thyme
1/2 tsp. oregano

1/2 tsp. Old Bay
1/2 tbsp. salt
1/2 tsp. white pepper
12 oz. V-8 juice
1/2 lb. whitefish
1/2 lb. crabmeat
1/2 lb. shrimp
1 lb. chopped clams
28 oz. can diced tomatoes
1 qt. gallon cream

Dice vegetables. Saute bacon and add vegetables, saute. Add flour and make a roux. Add fish stock and simmer until thickened. Add seasonings. Simmer. Add seafood to soup. Simmer about 10 minutes. Add cream to finish. Add potatoes last so as not to overcook.

Packy's Pub
General Manager/Chef Charlie Mayer

PACKY'S SEAFOOD SALAD

3 oz. cooked shrimp
3 oz. cooked scallops
3 oz. jumbo lump crabmeat
1 tsp. fresh chopped dill
1/4 c. mayonnaise
1 tsp. juice of fresh lemon
Dash of Tabasco

1 tsp. Worcestershire sauce
1/2 lb. fresh washed spinach,
  stems picked
1 tsp. white wine
1/2 tsp. capers
Salt and pepper to taste

Mix everything in bowl except seafood until smooth and consistent. Add seafood and serve on top of spinach. Serves 1.

Packy's Pub
Head Chef Matthew Thompson

SPRINGTIME LAMB STEW

To make this good-looking party stew, we've used an innovative French technique that calls for some new rules. As a first step, instead of browning the meat in oil, you "sweat" out the meat's natural juices. Next, boil the juices away, then neatly brown the meat in the rendered drippings. This technique turns out tender braised meat accompanied by a silken sauce.

3 lb. boneless lamb stew meat
  (neck or shoulder), cut into 1
  to 2-inch chunks
2 tbsp. soy sauce
1/2 c. Madeira or port
4 tsp. mustard seeds
1 tsp. thyme leaves
1/4 tsp. black peppercorns
2 bay leaves
1 1/2 c. regular strength chicken
  broth
1 c. dry red or white wine
1 1/2 to 2 lb. lb. sm. red or white
  thin-skinned potatoes,
  halved

8 to 12 slender carrots, peeled
3 to 6 sm. turnips, peeled and
  halved
6 to 12 sm. white boiling onions,
  peeled
3/4 lb. green beans, cut in half,
  ends and strings removed
1/2 pt. (1 c.) whipping cream
1 tbsp. Dijon mustard
Watercress

Place meat in a 5 or 6-quart Dutch oven. Stir in soy sauce. Cover and bring to a boil over medium heat; reduce heat and let meat simmer in its accumulated juices for 30 minutes. Remove lid and turn heat to high to boil juices down completely, about 10 minutes.

When meat starts to sizzle in its own fat, stir frequently until meat is richly browned. Add Madeira and stir well; then add mustard seeds, thyme, peppercorns, bay leaves, broth, and wine.

Lay potatoes, carrots, turnips, and onions on meat. Bring to a boil; cover, reduce heat, and let simmer for about 1 hour or until meat and vegetables are fork-tender.

After about 50 minutes, bring 1 inch water to a boil in a 2 to 3-quart pan. Drop in beans and cook, uncovered, until fork-tender, 5 to 8 minutes. Drain.

With a slotted spoon, lift vegetables and meat from broth and mound individually in a wide, shallow, ovenproof serving container. Arrange beans alongside other vegetables. Cover loosely with foil and keep hot in a 150 degree oven for as long as 20 minutes.

Meanwhile, remove bay leaves from pan juices; add cream and Dijon mustard. Boil on highest heat until sauce is golden, thickened slightly, and reduced to 1 3/4 cups, 8 to 10 minutes. Pour sauce into a serving container. Garnish meat and vegetables with watercress. Let guests serve themselves, spooning sauce onto individual portions. Makes 6 to 8 servings.

Ingleneuk Teahouse
Proprietor/Head Chef Scott Perrine

RED BURGUNDY MUSHROOM SOUP

1/4 c. (1/2 stick) butter
1 lb. flat mushrooms, sliced
2 onions, chopped
2 lg. potatoes, diced
1/2 c. red wine

1 1/2 c. beef stock
1 tsp. ground nutmeg
2 c. milk
Freshly ground black pepper

Melt 3 tablespoons butter in a heavy saucepan. Add 3/4 of the mushrooms and all the onions and cook for 5 minutes. Stir in potatoes, wine, stock and nutmeg. Bring to the boil, reduce heat and simmer for 15 minutes.

Transfer soup to a food processor or blender and process until smooth. Pour in milk and return to saucepan. Heat gently until soup is hot.

Melt 1/2 tablespoon butter in skillet and cook remaining mushrooms for 4-5 minutes. Season to taste with pepper. Stir into hot mushroom soup and serve.

Ingleneuk Teahouse
Proprietor/Head Chef Scott Perrine

LENTILS, FETA, AND SUN-DRIED TOMATO SALAD

2 1/2 tbsp. extra virgin olive oil
1/4 tsp. fresh thyme
1/4 c. marinated sun-dried tomatoes, packed in oil, drained and chopped

1 c. lentils, picked over and rinsed
1/2 c. feta, crumbled

In a large bowl, whisk together oil, vinegar, thyme, tomatoes, salt and pepper to taste. Add lentils to large pot of boiling salted water. Reduce heat and simmer until tender, 20 minutes. Drain lentils. Serve with greens and toss dressing, feta and lentils. Serves 4.

Kathryn's Inn
Head Chef Jerry Gonzalez

CHICK-PEA SOUP

1 lb. chick-peas
1 tsp. salt
2 sprigs rosemary, wrapped and tied in cheesecloth
1 garlic clove, minced

4 anchovy fillets
2 tbsp. olive oil
2 tomatoes, peeled and diced
2 qt. chicken broth
1/2 c. tubettini

Soak the chick-peas for 3 hours. Cook the chick-peas with salt and rosemary until chick-peas are tender. Discard the rosemary and put chick-peas and liquid through a food mill. Saute the garlic and anchovies in oil. Stir in the tomatoes and add the hot chicken broth. Simmer for 25 minutes. Blend the chick-peas. Cook tubettini al dente. Stir into the soup. Simmer for 5 minutes. 4-6 servings.

Rosario's
Head Chef Akin Randle

NECTARINES WITH PROSCIUTTO

Greens of your choice
2 nectarines
4 oz. thinly sliced Prosciutto
5 tbsp. sunflower oil

1 tbsp. raspberry vinegar
Fresh raspberries
3 tbsp. virgin olive oil

Line four plates with greens. Slice nectarines. Wrap each nectarine slice with Prosciutto; arrange on top of greens. Whisk together olive oil, sunflower oil and vinegar. Drizzle over salad. Garnish with raspberries and serve. 4 servings.

Rosario's
Head Chef Akin Randle

MIXED GARDEN GREENS WITH HERBED BLUEBERRY VINAIGRETTE

4 c. torn mixed greens
1 c. sliced fresh mushrooms
2 apples, cored and sliced

1/2 c. herbed blueberry
   vinaigrette
Fresh basil

In a large mixing bowl, combine mixed greens and mushrooms. Toss lightly to mix. Divide salad in 4 plates. Top each plate with apple slices.

HERBED BLUEBERRY VINAIGRETTE:

In a food processor, combine:

1/2 c. fresh blueberries
1/4 c. wine vinegar
1/2 tsp. sugar

1/8 tsp. pepper
Dash of salt

Cover and blend. In jar, combine the mixture with 3 tablespoons salad oil and 2 teaspoons chopped fresh basil. Cover and shake well and chill at least 1 hour. 4 servings.

Rosario's
Head Chef Akin Randle

GAZPACHO

3 lg. tomatoes, peeled and seeded
3 c. tomato juice
1/4 c. olive oil
1 med. onion
1 red bell pepper
1 lg. cucumber, peeled and
　seeded

1/3 c. red wine vinegar
1/3 c. fresh cilantro, chopped
2 jalapeno peppers, seeded
Salt and pepper

Rough chop 2 tomatoes, 1/2 cucumber, jalapenos, 1/2 onion and 1/2 red pepper. Puree in food processor and transfer to mixing bowl. Add tomato juice, olive oil, vinegar and cilantro. Fine dice remaining tomato, cucumber, onion and red pepper and add to soup. Add salt and pepper to taste. Chill for several hours before serving.

Dugal's Inn
Head Chef/Proprietor Scott Nyman

RASPBERRY-POPPY SEED VINAIGRETTE

Choice of fresh greens and
　vegetables
1/2 c. raspberry vinegar
1/4 c. honey

1 c. olive oil
1 tbsp. poppy seeds
1/4 tsp. granulated garlic

In mixing bowl, combine all ingredients except oil and greens and mix well. Slowly add oil while whisking to incorporate. Toss greens in desired amount of dressing.

Dugal's Inn
Chef Geoff Young

RABBIT SOUP

1 rabbit, cubed
2 celery stalks, sliced
1 lg. onion, chopped
4 sliced carrots
3 lg. potatoes, cubed
2 turnips, cubed
3 tbsp. butter

1 tsp. grated lemon rind
Pinch of mace
1/2 gallon chicken broth
1 c. wide noodles
2 tbsp. minced basil
2 tbsp. minced thyme
2 tbsp. mixed cilantro

In a large kettle, add celery, onion, carrots, potato, turnips, rabbit, basil, thyme, cilantro, butter. Saute for 10 minutes. Add chicken broth, mace, lemon rind. Bring to boil. Simmer for 20 minutes. Add noodles and cook until tender.

Septembers Place
Executive Chef John Birmingham

WARM RED CABBAGE SALAD

2 tsp. pine nuts
2 tbsp. vegetable oil
2 tbsp. balsamic vinegar
1/2 tbsp. sugar
Salt and pepper

2 tbsp. bacon bits
1 lb. cooked, julienned chicken breast
1 1/2 lb. shredded red cabbage
1/4 c. Roquefort cheese

In a saute pan, add oil, balsamic vinegar, sugar, and cabbage. Saute for 5 minutes. Add bacon, pine nuts, and toss. Remove to plate. Top with chicken and Roquefort. Serves 2.

Septembers Place
Executive Chef John Birmingham

ZUCCHINI-PARMESAN SOUP WITH ROASTED RED PEPPERS

2 1/2 tbsp. butter
1/2 c. onion, diced finely
1 clove garlic, minced
3 tbsp. flour
2 c. chicken stock

3/4 c. milk
3 tbsp. grated Parmesan cheese
1/4 c. roasted red pepper, diced
Pinch of white pepper
Thyme leaves to taste

Melt butter in a heavy duty saucepan. Add onions and saute until just transparent. Add garlic and saute 30 seconds. Add flour and whisk for 1 minute over medium heat. Add chicken stock, whisk and bring to a boil. Add zucchini. Simmer 4 minutes, add milk. Whisk in Parmesan cheese and roasted peppers. Season to taste.

O'Flagherty's
Chef Mark Chopko

SPINACH SALAD WITH SMOKED TURKEY
(AND AN ORANGE VINAIGRETTE DRESSING)

SALAD:

5 oz. fresh spinach, picked and
  washed
4 oz. smoked turkey, cut lg. and
  julienned
2 med. fresh mushrooms, sliced
1/8 med. red onion, thinly sliced
  julienne

1/2 orange, cut in 4 slices
1/2 blood orange, cut in 4 slices
1/8 red pepper, cut thinly into
  julienne strips
1/8 yellow pepper, cut thinly
  into julienne strips

Place spinach in salad bowl, then top with mushrooms, red onions. Then place turkey in a circle from middle of bowl to outer rim. Place orange halves around edge alternating blood and navel oranges. Sprinkle red and green peppers on the top and add vinaigrette dressing to taste. Yields: 1 serving.

ORANGE VINAIGRETTE DRESSING:

1 tbsp. frozen orange juice
  concentrate
1 tbsp. white vinegar

1/4 tsp. basil
Salt and pepper to taste
3 tbsp. canola oil

O'Flagherty's
Chef Mark Chopko

TOMATO PEPPER ONION SALAD

3 lg. tomatoes
2 med. green peppers
1 onion, sliced thin
12 tbsp. olive oil

Salt
Lemon pepper
Garlic salt

Core and dice tomatoes, clean and dice peppers and sliced onion and combine in bowl with olive oil. Season to taste with salt, lemon pepper and garlic salt.

Palumbo's Edgmont Inn
Executive Head Chef Richard Hudson

PASTA SALAD WITH BROCCOLI AND TUNA

1 bunch fresh broccoli, tops cut
    into bite-size florets, stems
    cut into bite-size pieces
1 lb. rigatoni
2 c. (3/4 lg.) sliced scallions
1 1/2 lb. (3/4 lg.) fresh tomatoes,
    cut into wedges
2 (7 oz.) cans tuna, packed in
    olive oil, drained and
    coarsely flaked

3 garlic cloves, minced
3 tbsp. finely chopped Italian
    flat leaf parsley
2 tbsp. chopped fresh basil
1/2 c. olive oil
1 tsp. salt
1/2 tsp. black pepper

In a large saucepan of rapidly boiling salted water, cook the broccoli until crisp-tender but still green, 2 to 3 minutes. Remove with a slotted spoon or skinner and rinse under cold water. Add the pasta to the same water and cook until tender but still firm, 12 to 15 minutes.

Drain, rinse in cold water, drain again and pour into a large serving bowl. Add the scallions, tomatoes, tuna, garlic, parsley, basil, olive oil, salt and pepper to the pasta and toss lightly. Do not refrigerate this dish. Serve at room temperature. Yield: 8 to 10 servings.

Trieste Restaurant
Head Chef Richard Day

MANHATTAN STYLE CLAM CHOWDER

1 c. potatoes, peeled and chopped
1 2/3 c. water
2 (1 lb.) cans tomatoes, chopped
1 c. celery, chopped
2/3 c. green pepper, chopped
1 (10 oz.) pkg. frozen cut green
    beans, thawed
1 tbsp. margarine
1 1/2 c. clam juice

1/4 c. bacon bits
2 tbsp. catsup
1 tbsp. Worcestershire sauce
1 1/2 tsp. Italian herbs
1/4 tsp. basil
2 bay leaves
Salt and pepper to taste
1 c. clams, finely chopped
1/4 tsp. thyme

In a large saucepan, boil potatoes in water for 10 minutes. Add remaining ingredients except clams. Allow to simmer on medium-low heat for 45 minutes. Add clams and simmer for 5 more minutes.

Trieste Restaurant
Head Chef Richard Day

LANGOSTINO, ARTICHOKE HEART SALAD

1 c. shelled langostino
3 c. artichoke hearts, halved
1/2 c. garbanzo beans
1/4 c. minced shallots
1/2 c. diced jicama
1 head Belgian endive

1/2 c. olive oil (Pomace)
1/4 c. sherry wine vinegar
2 tbsp. lime juice
2 tbsp. sugar
2 tbsp. pickling spice

Poach langostino in pickling spice and chill. Combine artichoke hearts, shallots, jicama, garbanzo beans and mix evenly.

In small mixing bowl, incorporate olive oil, sherry vinegar, lime juice and sugar to make dressing. Add chilled langostino to artichoke salad and toss thoroughly but gently with dressing. Lay 5 Belgian endive leaves on two separate round plates and place salad over leaves. Serves 2.

NOTE: Do not use extra virgin or virgin olive oil because taste would overpower the dressing.

Rossi's Town Inn
Executive Chef Chris Buonopane

SHRIMP NICOISE SALAD

1 lb. (25-30) shrimp, shelled, deveined
1 1/2 c. whole button mushrooms
1 med. Vidalia onion, julienne
2 red bell peppers, julienne
1 c. nicoise olives

1 c. mayonnaise
1/4 c. red wine vinegar
3 tbsp. Dijon mustard
2 tbsp. honey
2 tbsp. sugar
4 whole wheat pita shells
Salt and pepper

Poach shrimp, set aside to chill. Combine mushrooms, onions, peppers and olives. Mix mayonnaise, vinegar, mustard, honey and sugar to make dressing. Add chilled shrimp to salad and toss thoroughly with dressing. Salt and pepper to taste and toss again. Divide salad evenly into 1/4's and lace over pita shells. Serves 4.

Rossi's Town Inn
Executive Chef Chris Buonopane

CRAB AND WHITE ASPARAGUS BISQUE

1 lb. backfin crabmeat, picked
1 lg. onion, diced sm.
4 celery stalks, diced sm.
1 carrot, grated
2 (12 oz.) cans white asparagus
1 qt. clam juice
1 qt. heavy cream

2 tbsp. fresh dill
1/4 c. salt
2 tbsp. black pepper
1 qt. water
2/3 c. cornstarch
8 oz. butter

Saute onions and celery in butter until translucent. Add clam juice, water, salt, pepper, dill and carrots. Bring to a rolling boil. Dice asparagus into 1-inch pieces and add with brine from can. Add crabmeat and heavy cream. Stir so soup incorporates thoroughly and does not burn.

When soup starts to simmer, add 1/4 cup of cold water to starch. Form paste and add to soup to thicken.

NOTE: Once cream is added to soup, do not let soup come to a full boil.

Rossi's Town Inn
Executive Chef Chris Buonopane

BLACKENED DUCK, BLACK BEAN SOUP

2 (4 oz.) duck breasts
1 med. onion, diced sm.
4 celery stalks, diced sm.
1 green pepper, diced sm.
3 garlic cloves, minced
1 lb. black beans
2 tbsp. lemon zest
3 c. water for beans
1 qt. water

2 qt. brown chicken stock
1 carrot, sliced thin
Sour cream
1/2 c. salt
1 tbsp. white pepper
1/2 c. Cajun seasoning
1 c. white wine
8 oz. butter

Boil 3 cups water, add beans and let stand for 2 hours with covered lid. Tenderize duck breasts and coat both sides with Cajun seasoning. Blacken in iron skillet and slice into small thin pieces. Deglaze pan with wine and add to chicken stock.

In pot, saute onions, celery, garlic in butter until translucent. Add water, stock, beans, lemon zest, pepper, white pepper and salt. Cook over moderate heat, stirring frequently for 1/2 hour. Add carrots. Cook until beans are tender but firm. Add breast meat. Serve with a dollop of fresh sour cream in the center.

NOTE: Brown chicken stock can be made by roasting chicken bones before boiling.

Rossi's Town Inn
Executive Chef Chris Buonopane

LENTIL SOUP WITH HAM

10 c. chicken stock
2 lg. onions
1 1/2 c. minced celery

2 lb. ham butt
1 1/2 c. dried lentils

In a large saucepan, combine the stock, onion, carrot, celery and ham. Cover and simmer for 1 hour. Remove the ham. Add the lentils and simmer until tender, about 40 to 45 minutes. Skin and bone ham, then cut the meat into chunks. Add the ham to the soup and heat. Season to taste with pepper. Serves 6.

Pike Family Restaurant
Chef Robert Kellock

OYSTER STEW

4 c. half & half
1 qt. fresh oyster with juice

1/4 c. butter
Salt and pepper

In large heavy saucepan, heat half & half over low heat. Add the oyster and let simmer over low heat until the mixture starts to boil. Do not let boil. Stir in the remaining ingredients except salt and pepper. Stir until butter melts. Season to taste with salt and pepper. Serves 6.

Pike Family Restaurant
Chef Robert Kellock

CREAM OF CARROT SOUP GARNISHED WITH CINNAMON STICKS

The bright orange color and bright flavor distinguish this carrot soup from the ordinary. It is excellent hot or cold.

1 sm. peeled, chopped onion
10 carrots, peeled, sliced thin
1 c. dry sherry

1/4 lb. sweet butter
1 1/2 qt. heavy cream
4 chicken bouillon cubes

In a saucepan, slowly melt butter, add onions and brown slightly. Add carrots, stir constantly and let cook for 15 minutes. Add sherry and bouillon cubes and let boil, stirring constantly. Add cream and bring to rolling boil until carrots are very soft. Take off heat and puree. Heat before serving. Add cinnamon sticks as garnish.

Bobby's Seafood Restaurant
Executive Chef Bob Donovan

ZUCCHINI CURRY SOUP WITH CRAB

5 zucchini, washed, ends
   removed, and grated
1 med. onion, diced
1 1/2 c. dry sherry
1 c. ground curry

1/4 lb. sweet butter
1 c. chicken consomme
1 1/2 qt. heavy cream
1/2 lb. jumbo lump crabmeat

In a saucepan, caramelize onions until slightly brown. Add zucchini and curry. Cook mixture until curry flavor begins to get pungent. Deglaze with sherry, reduce by half. Add consomme, heavy cream and bring to a rolling boil. Add salt and pepper to taste, finish with crabmeat.

Bobby's Seafood Restaurant
Executive Chef Bob Donovan

RADICCHIO VINAIGRETTE

1 sm. head Radicchio lettuce
1 head Romaine
1 tomato
1 cucumber
1/2 c. baked croutons

1/4 c. virgin olive oil
1/4 c. balsamic vinegar
1 tsp. crushed garlic
Salt and pepper to taste
1 tsp. granulated garlic

Wash lettuce and drain well. Place in large wooden bowl. Cut tomatoes into wedges and cucumber slices. Add to lettuce, add in croutons. Pour in oil and vinegar and crushed garlic. Sprinkle top of salad with granulated garlic, salt and pepper. Don't be stingy with spices. Toss salad and serve. Serves 4.

Cafe Elana
Head Chef/Proprietor Dominic Ventura

SEAFOOD CHOWDER WHITE OR RED

1 lb. flounder
1 lb. shrimp
1 lb. scallops
1/2 lb. crabmeat
1 qt. cubed potatoes
1 sliced onion

1 1/2 inch cubed fat-salt pork
1 tbsp. salt
1/8 tsp. pepper
3 tbsp. butter
4 c. scalded milk
8 cracker crumbs

Cut flounder, shrimp, scallops and crab in small pieces and set aside. Cut salt pork in small pieces. Add onion and fry 5 minutes; strain fat into large pan. Add potatoes to fat, then add 2 cups boiling water and cook 5 minutes. Add fish and cover and simmer 10 minutes. Add milk, salt, pepper and butter. Cook 5 minutes. Serve with cracker crumbs on bottom of bowl. Serves 8.

If you want red, omit milk. Add 2 1/2 cups of stewed and strained tomatoes.

Cafe Elana
Sous Chef Jeanne Sarne

CUCUMBER CARROT SALAD

2 seedless cucumbers, quartered
   lengthwise, seeded, and
   cored
1 carrot, peeled and shredded
2 tbsp. fresh lime juice
1 tsp. garlic, chopped
1 tbsp. sugar

1 1/2 tbsp. fish sauce (available
   in grocery store)
Serrano or thai pepper, seeded
   and diced (do not touch eyes,
   lips or skin with pepper)
Mixed greens for bed under
   salad

In a wooden or glass bowl, mix garlic, lime, fish sauce, sugar, and pepper. Allow sugar to dissolve. Slice cucumbers thin, add to garlic, mix with carrots. Serve on greens and toss before serving. Serves 6.

Kathryn's Inn
Head Chef Jerry Gonzalez

5 GREENS SOUP

2 1/2 lb. greens (collard greens,
    Romaine, escarole, mustard
    and caraway)
2 qt. chicken stock
2 tbsp. garlic, chopped

1 c. white wine
1 c. ricotta cheese
1/2 c. sour cream
Salt and pepper

Clean and wash greens, cut off ends and stems. Drain thoroughly. Put greens in soup pot with stock and garlic. Bring pot to a boil, then cover. Lower heat and simmer until greens are tender. Strain off greens (saving liquids). Blend greens in food processor, but don't puree.

In a large pot, combine 3 cups of reserved stock, and the rest of the ingredients, except salt and pepper. Simmer 20 minutes. Stir with wooden spoon occasionally. Season to taste with salt and pepper. Makes 9-10 cups.

Kathryn's Inn
Head Chef Jerry Gonzalez

GROCERY SALAD/CHAMPAGNE VINAIGRETTE

1 1/4 each anchovy filet
1/2 tbsp. garlic
1/2 tbsp. shallots
3/4 tbsp. Dijon mustard
1/2 tbsp. lemon juice

1 egg
1/8 c. red wine vinegar
1/8 c. grated locatelli
1/2 tbsp. parsley
Salt and pepper to taste

Place all ingredients in food processor and blend.

1 3/4 c. olive oil

Stream into above until thick and creamy.

1/4 c. champagne

Add to above and blend.

2 lb. cleaned and dried spinach,
    stems removed
1/4 lb. sun-dried tomatoes
1 lb. marinated artichoke hearts,
    quartered

1/2 lb. Gorgonzola cheese, cut
    into cubes
2 roasted red peppers, cut into
    strips

Set aside.

To serve: Place spinach in large mixing bowl, add enough dressing and mix, to coat spinach. Arrange coated spinach on 8 serving plates, distribute remaining ingredients evenly on top of spinach and serve. Serves 8.

Cafe Nola
Executive Chef Marco Carrozza
Chef de Cuisine Tom Downing

PASTA AND CHICK PEA SOUP

1 1/2 qt. chicken broth
4 oz. Prosciutto, chopped
1 can chick peas, drained
2 c. ditallini
Chopped parsley
2 tbsp. olive oil

2 cloves garlic, chopped
4 oz. strained tomatoes
2 fillets anchovies
Pinch of rosemary
1 sm. onion, chopped

In a medium saucepan, boil the chicken broth with the chick peas, strained tomatoes and pasta.
In another pan, heat the oil. Saute the garlic, Prosciutto, onion and anchovy fillets for 6 to 8 minutes or until the vegetables are tender. Add the sauteed vegetables to the broth. Stir occasionally. Boil the soup for a few minutes longer. Serve and sprinkle with cheese and parsley.

Scampi
Proprietor/Chef Joseph P. Kirkwood

HERBED TOMATO AND PASTA SALAD

8 oz. penne pasta
1 lb. ripe tomatoes, peeled,
   seeded, and quartered
6 scallions, chopped

1 garlic clove, crushed
Salt and fresh ground pepper
4-6 tbsp. olive oil
6 basil sprigs

Cook pasta in boiling salted water for 3 minutes. Drain, set aside to cool. Mix the tomatoes with the scallions and set aside to cool.
Mix the tomatoes with the scallions. Add the garlic, seasoning and olive oil, and mix well. Cover and set aside to marinate for 1 hour. Toss the tomato mixture into the paste, chop basil, Mix well and serve at once.

Scampi
Proprietor/Chef Joseph P. Kirkwood

SCRATHATELLI SOUP

1 qt. homemade chicken stock
8 oz. chopped, cooked spinach
1 med. ripe tomato, seeded and
    diced

2 eggs, beaten lightly
Salt and pepper
Romano cheese to taste

Bring chicken broth to a boil. Add spinach, tomato, salt, pepper and cheese. Return to boil. Add eggs by drizzling from tines of fork. Serve immediately. Serves 4 people.

Scampi
Mark Cugini

BROCCOLI AND CHEESE SOUP

1 bunch broccoli
1/2 gallon water
1 qt. milk

1/2 lb. cheddar cheese
Pinch of white pepper
2 oz. chicken base

Bring water, milk, pepper and chicken base to a boil. Mix in grated cheddar cheese. Thicken with flour and water, mix. Add broccoli. Simmer for 10 minutes. Serves 6 to 10.

Fireside
Head Chef Adolph Funches

SHRIMP BISQUE

COURT BOUILLONS:

1 gallon water
1/2 lb. onion, chopped fine
1 lemon, thin sliced

1 bay leaf
3 whole cloves
4 oz. celery, chopped fine

2 lb. raw shrimp in shell

ROUX:

1 lb. butter
12 oz. flour

2 tsp. paprika

2 qt. hot milk
1 qt. light hot cream

4 oz. sherry wine

Combine water, onion, lemon, bay leaf, cloves, and celery. Simmer 15 minutes. Strain liquid into soup pot, bring to a boil. Add raw shrimp and simmer 5 to 6 minutes. Remove shrimp from stock (court bouillon) and reserve stock.

Cool shrimp in cold water, peel and devein. Coarsely chop and reserve.

Make a roux with butter, flour and paprika, blending well. Cook 3 to 4 minutes. Do not burn. Add hot stock slowly, stirring until thickened and smooth. Add combined milk and cream. Add sherry and shrimp. Season to taste.

Seven Stars Inn
Head Chef Michael Walters

TUNA SESAME WITH BABY GREENS AND SHRIMP SALAD

1 (8 oz.) tuna filet, cut in 3
    triangles
6 oz. white sesame seeds
3 oz. flour

1 lemon
1 egg
1 tbsp. sesame oil or butter
Salt and pepper

SALAD:

4 oz. spring mix
3 cherry tomatoes, cut in
    quarters

1 hard-boiled egg, cut in quarters
4 shrimp, peeled and deveined
1 roasted pepper, sliced

DRESSING:

1 tbsp. honey
1 tbsp. hoisin sauce
1 tbsp. balsamic vinegar
1 tsp. rice vinegar
1 oz. sesame oil

1/2 garlic clove, chopped
1 tsp. fresh ginger
Pinch of cayenne pepper
Salt and pepper

TUNA: For the tuna, cut in 3 triangles. Salt and pepper to taste. Squeeze lemon in flour and shake off excess. Coat in egg, then crust with sesame seeds. Saute tuna and shrimp on medium heat in sesame oil until brown on both sides. Reserve tuna and shrimp.

DRESSING: For dressing, mix all ingredients together in bowl.

SALAD: Take 4 oz. spring mix, roll in dressing with shrimp.

ARRANGEMENT: Put salad and shrimp on plate. Arrange tuna in "Y" form. Garnish with cherry tomatoes, egg and roasted pepper.

Rose Tree Inn
Head Chef John Schatz

CHICKEN ANGELIQUE

2 lb. chicken tenders, cooked, poached
3/4 c. mayonnaise
1 tbsp. lemon juice
1/4 tsp. salt
Pinch of fresh green pepper

1 tbsp. white wine
2 tbsp. fresh tarragon
1/2 c. toasted almond slivers
1 bunch scallions, bias cut
2 ribs celery, sm. dice

Poach chicken tenders or breasts in chicken stock until just done. Cool in refrigerator.

In the meantime, combine all other ingredients in a bowl. Mix with chicken when it is cool. Store in refrigerator until you are ready to eat.

Thyme Catering
Christine Amarosa Neugebauer, C.W.C.

CHICKEN AND WHOLE WHEAT NOODLES WITH ASPARAGUS AND SESAME DRESSING

1/2 c. tamari ginger sauce
1/2 c. water
1 tbsp. dry sherry
1 tbsp. grated ginger
1/2 c. chopped scallions
1 sm. clove crushed garlic
2 tsp. sesame oil
2 tsp. red vinegar

2 tsp. sugar
1 lb. whole wheat noodles
1 lb. asparagus
1 lb. chicken breast
2 c. julienne carrots
1/2 c. scallions
3 tbsp. toasted sesame seeds

Combine first nine ingredients to make sauce. Cook noodles al dente. Roast chicken breasts. Poach asparagus, then slice on bias.

Combine 3/4 of sauce and all ingredients except chicken and sesame seeds. Put noodle salad in a nice bowl. Slice chicken on a bias. Layer chicken over noodles. Sprinkle with sesame seeds and chopped scallions. 8-10 servings.

Thyme Catering
Christine Amarosa Neugebauer, C.W.C.

MEDITERRANEAN SEAFOOD SALAD

1 lb. shrimp
1 lb. crabmeat
1/2 lb. scallops
1 red bell pepper

1 green bell pepper
1 yellow bell pepper
3 scallions
1 head red leafy lettuce

VINAIGRETTE:

3 oz. balsamic vinegar
6 oz. V-8 juice
12 oz. olive oil
1 clove garlic, chopped fine

1 bunch julienne fresh basil
1 tsp. salt
1 tsp. fresh ground pepper

Combine Vinaigrette. Cook, peel, devein the shrimp. Pick crab from shells. Poach scallops just done. Small dice peppers. Cut scallions on a bias. Combine above ingredients. Add vinaigrette to taste. Serve cold on lettuce-leafy red. 8-10 servings.

Thyme Catering
Christine Amarosa Neugebauer, C.W.C.

PINEAPPLE-RAISIN WALDORF SALAD

1 lb. apples
4 oz. raisins
8 oz. celery, diced fine
4 oz. canned pineapple, diced, drained

Mayonnaise to bind
2 heads lettuce, washed, trimmed
3 oz. walnuts, chopped

Pare washed apples partially, leaving portion of red skin. Core and dice. Place in juice from pineapple. Plump raisins in steamer or hot water. Drain well and dry on clean towels. All ingredients must be dry.

Combine apples, raisins, celery and pineapple. Mix with mayonnaise to bind. Serve in lettuce cups and garnish with chopped walnuts.

Seven Stars Inn
Head Chef Michael Walters

CREAM OF 4 MUSHROOM SOUP

1/2 lb. button mushrooms, sliced
1/4 lb. shiitake mushrooms, sliced
1/4 lb. cremini mushrooms, sliced
1/4 lb. portobella mushrooms, sliced
2 oz. dried porcini mushrooms (reconstituted in 1/4 c. hot water)

1 med. white onion, diced
2 cloves minced garlic
1 bay leaf
Pinch of thyme
2 c. chicken stock
Salt and pepper
1/4 lb. sweet butter
4 tbsp. arrow root
1 1/2 qt. heavy cream
2 sprigs fresh dill, diced

In 6-quart saucepan, sweat onion and mushrooms, bay leaf and thyme. Add reserved porcini liquid and chicken stock. Reduce by 2/3's. Add 1 quart cream and bring to a boil. Thicken with arrow root slowly. Add remaining cream and whole butter. Season with salt and pepper and fresh dill. Serves 6.

American Bistro
Executive Head Chef James E. Webb

CUCUMBER APPLE SOUP

2 lg. cucumber, peeled and
   seeded
2 green apples, peeled and seeded
1 sm. red onion
2 c. chicken stock, reduced to 1/4
   c. and chilled
2 sprigs dill, diced

2 tbsp. chopped chives
1/4 c. sour cream
1/4 c. yogurt
1 pt. heavy cream
Salt and pepper
Juice of 1 lemon
1 tbsp. rice wine vinegar

In food processor, puree cucumber, apples and onion. Transfer to bowl. Whisk in stock, dill, chives, sour cream, yogurt, heavy cream, lemon and vinegar. Season with salt and pepper. Serve chilled. Serves 6.

American Bistro
Executive Head Chef James E. Webb

GASPACHO

6 lg. cucumbers, peeled and
   minced
2 oz. salt
1 1/2 qt. tomatoes
4 oz. pimentos
6 green onions, minced
2 oz. vinegar
2 oz. olive oil

1 clove garlic, minced
1 tbsp. sugar
1/4 tsp. cumin
Salt and pepper to taste
2 qt. water
Consomme, if desired
Chives, chopped for garnish

Wash cucumber, add salt. Let stand several minutes. Add tomatoes, pimentos and onions. Mix together vinegar, oil, garlic, sugar, cumin, salt and pepper. Let stand for several minutes. Add to cucumber mixture. Combine all ingredients. Chill well and garnish with chopped chives.

Seven Stars Inn
Head Chef Michael Walters

JAPANESE CLAM SOUP

1/4 oz. dried mushrooms
2 oz. bamboo shoots
10 pieces snow peas
Boiling chicken stock
2 oz. sherry wine

1/8 tsp. white pepper
1/4 tsp. salt
1 (10 1/2 oz.) can Japanese baby
   clams
10 lemon slices

Wash mushrooms in cold water. Drain well. Chop mushrooms, julienne bamboo shoots. Place mushrooms, bamboo shoots and snow peas in boiling stock. Simmer about 4 minutes. Add remaining ingredients, bring back to a boil and remove from heat. Adjust seasonings and serve with lemon slices.

Seven Stars Inn
Head Chef Michael Walters

NEW ENGLAND CLAM CHOWDER

1 onion	1/2 gallon water
4 stalks celery	1 bay leaf
1 can chopped clams	4 oz. clam base
1/2 gallon milk	2 diced potatoes

Mix all ingredients in large pot. Cook for 1/2 hour. Add flour and water mixture. Simmer until done. 10 servings.

Fireside
Head Chef Adolph Funches

SPLIT PEA SOUP

1 lb. split peas	2 oz. ham base
1 gallon water	1/4 lb. ham, diced

Cook split peas in water for 45 minutes. Add ham base. Simmer for 20 minutes. 8 servings.

Fireside
Head Chef Adolph Funches

COUS COUS SALAD WITH DRIED TOMATO BASIL VINAIGRETTE

DRESSING:

1/3 c. olive oil
3 tbsp. red wine vinegar
1 tsp. dried oregano
1/4 tsp. salt
1/8 tsp. cayenne

1 tbsp. roasted mustard seed
1 tbsp. roasted cumin seed
1/3 c. dried tomato, minced
1/3 c. fresh basil

BASIL VINAIGRETTE SALAD:

1 1/2 lb. mixed greens
1 med. red bell pepper
3 c. water
1/4 tsp. salt
1/4 tsp. garlic powder

1 tbsp. butter
2 c. dried cous cous
1 med. peeled, seeded cucumber
1/4 c. red onion, minced

Mix dressing well in advance. Mix olive oil, vinegar, oregano, salt, cayenne, dried tomato. Place mustard seed and cumin seed in a heavy saute pan and place on medium heat until golden, stirring frequently.

When golden brown, place in olive oil mixture; it will sizzle. Add fresh basil, cover and set aside.

Place water, salt, garlic powder, and butter in a sauce pot; bring to a boil. Add cous cous, cover and remove from heat. Roast bell pepper in broiler section of oven until skin is black. Place in a freezer bag and chill. Remove skin.

Mix grated cucumber and minced onion in a bowl and julienne roasted pepper. Add dressing and cous cous, tossing to distribute evenly. Place on mixed greens and enjoy. Yields: 6 side dishes.

Evviva
Chef Larry E. Langley-Ward

RASPBERRY VINAIGRETTE

1 pt. raspberries (strawberries
   can be substituted)
1/4 c. balsamic vinegar
4 tbsp. sugar (3 packets of Sweet
   'n Low instead of sugar can
   be used)

1 tbsp. shallots
1 tbsp. basil
1/2 c. olive oil

Heat raspberries, balsamic vinegar, sugar, and chopped shallots over medium heat. Reduce until slightly thickened, remove from heat and add basil; refrigerate until cooled.

Place mixture in a food processor and blend for 1 1/2 minutes. Strain mixture using fine strainer and place back in processor. Again, blend and slowly add olive oil in a stream. Turn machine off. If too thick, add more vinegar to taste. Add salt and pepper and serve over favorite greens.

Evviva
Chef Larry E. Langley-Ward

NEW ENGLAND CLAM CHOWDER

2 med. onions, med. diced
2 green peppers, med. diced
4 stalks celery, med. diced
3 raw potatoes, med. diced
1 lb. melted butter
1 lb. flour
1 (32 oz.) can chopped clams,
   drain juice and save

1 qt. heavy cream
2 tbsp. oregano
1 tbsp. thyme
1 tbsp. basil
Salt and pepper to taste

Saute onion, celery, peppers and potatoes in butter until transparent. Add flour and cook over medium heat for 8-10 minutes. Add hot clam juice to pot and cook until smooth. Add heavy cream, spices and salt and pepper to taste. Serves 4 to 6.

Palumbo's Edgmont Inn
Executive Chef Richard Hudson

EXTRA RECIPES

Vegetables

PARSLEY

VARIOUS VEGGIE TIPS

Bake potatoes in half the usual time by letting stand in boiling water for 15 minutes before putting them into a very hot oven.

Overcooked potatoes can become soggy when the milk is added. Sprinkle with dry powdered milk for the fluffiest mashed potatoes ever.

Plant a few sprigs of dill near your tomato plants to prevent tomato worms on your plants.

Exposure to direct sunlight softens tomatoes instead of ripening them. Leave the tomatoes, stem-up, in any spot where they will be out of direct sunlight.

Next time you are cooking cabbage, put a heel of bread on top of cabbage before putting the lid on the pot - there will be NO odor. The bread has no effect on the cabbage and should be removed after cooking. Works for broccoli and brussel sprouts too.

A deep or rich color generally indicates highest food value and flavor in vegetables. For example, the dark green outer leaves of leafy vegetables have more nutrients than the lighter colored inner ones. Also, bright orange carrots may provide more vitamin A than paler ones.

Remember to remove the tops of carrots before storing. Tops drain the carrots of moisture, making them limp and dry.

You'll shed less tears if you cut the root end of the onion off last; or, freeze or refrigerate before chopping.

Beans are nutritional superstars. Packed with protein, low in fat and cholesterol, beans are one of the best sources of complex carbohydrates and dietary fiber. Surprisingly, beans contain more fiber per serving than most other vegetables, fruits, grains or cereals. A diet high in soluble fiber has been linked to such virtues as lowering cholesterol, maintaining blood sugar levels or body energy, and delaying feeling hungry.

Lettuce leaves absorb fat. Place a few into the pot and watch the fat cling to them.

Ripen green bananas or green tomatoes by wrapping them in a wet dish towel and placing them in a paper sack.

A squirt of lemon in the water when cooking cauliflower will keep the cauliflower from discoloring.

Cook carrots and potatoes and then mash them all together. This makes the potatoes a light orange color and produces an entirely new flavor.

Never immerse mushrooms in water when cleaning. They will absorb too much liquid. For prime mushrooms, buy only those with closed caps. The gills should not be showing.

Vegetables

FALL GRATIN OF POTATO, TURNIP AND DELICATA SQUASH

1 lb. yellow potatoes, peeled and
    sliced 3/4 inch thick
1 med. turnip, peeled and sliced
    3/4 inch thick
1 "Delicata" squash, peeled and
    sliced 3/4 inch thick
2 oz. butter

Salt
Pepper
Nutmeg
1 pt. heavy cream (the quantity
    depending on the size of the
    gratin dish)
1 clove garlic

Rub the gratin dish with the peeled clove of garlic and butter the dish with half the butter. Arrange the potato, turnip and squash in layers adding salt, pepper and a pinch of nutmeg to each layer. Pour over the cream just to cover. Blot with the remaining butter. Bake in a low oven for 1 to 1 1/2 hours increasing the heat 15 minutes before the end to brown the top.

Swiss Gruyere cheese can be added to give a different taste and look. Delicious with lamb roast or simply with a salad of lettuces.

The Restaurant 210 at the Rittenhouse
Sous Chef Thomas J. Harkins
James Coleman, Executive Chef

BACON AND CHEESE BRUSSEL SPROUTS

1 lb. Brussels sprouts, trimmed
1 1/4 c. grated cheddar cheese

2 slices bacon, chopped

Steam, boil or microwave sprouts until just tender. Drain and arrange in a shallow ovenproof dish. Sprinkle with cheese, bacon and a little cayenne pepper. Place under a preheated grill and cook until bacon is crisp and cheese is bubbling and brown.

Ingleneuk Teahouse
Proprietor/Head Chef Scott Perrine

POTATOES WITH HERBED CREAM CHEESE

4 lg. potatoes, scrubbed
2 tsp. olive oil
Fresh thyme, finely chopped
Freshly ground black pepper to
   taste

4 cloves garlic, peeled and cut in
   half

HERBED CREAM CHEESE:

3 oz. pkg. cream cheese
2 tbsp. finely chopped fresh
   herbs (parsley, thyme and
   chives)

Using an apple corer, carefully remove a plug from each potato, making sure not to go through the potato. Reserve the plugs.

Combine oil, thyme and pepper. Fill each hole in potato with 2 garlic halves and 1/2 teaspoon of oil mixture. Cut off 2/3 of the plug and discard. Replace remaining plug in potato. Bake at 400 degrees for 1 hour or until potatoes are tender.

To make Herbed Cream Cheese, mix together cream cheese and herbs and serve with potatoes.

Ingleneuk Teahouse
Proprietor/Head Chef Scott Perrine

LEMON ASPARAGUS CARROTS

1/2 lb. asparagus or 1 (8 oz.) pkg.
   frozen asparagus spears
1/2 lb. sm. carrots
Lemon juice

Lemon pepper
Lemon wedges (optional)
Snipped parsley (optional)

To prepare fresh asparagus, wash and scrape off scales. Snap off and discard the woody bases. Tie the whole asparagus spears in a bundle. Stand the bundle upright in a deep kettle, letting tips extend 2 to 3 inches above boiling salted water. Cover and cook for 10 to 15 minutes or until crisp-tender. (Or, cook frozen asparagus spears according to package directions.) Rinse the cooked asparagus spears in cold water; drain.

Meanwhile, to prepare carrots, wash, trim, and peel the small carrots. Place the carrots in a steamer basket above boiling water. Cover and steam about 15 minutes or until crisp-tender. Rinse the cooked carrots in cold water; drain.

Cover and chill the cooked and drained asparagus spears and carrots. To serve, arrange the asparagus spears and carrots on a serving platter. Sprinkle with a little lemon juice and lemon pepper. Garnish with lemon wedges and parsley, if desired. Makes 6 servings.

Ingleneuk Teahouse
Proprietor/Head Chef Scott Perrine

ROASTED GARLIC WHIPPED POTATOES

6 Idaho potatoes, peeled
1 gallon water
1 bulb garlic
1/2 c. butter

1 c. heavy cream
1 tbsp. olive oil
1/2 c. Parmesan cheese
Salt and pepper

In oven at 400 degrees, roast garlic bulb for 20 minutes. Remove and let cool. Remove garlic pulp from skin and reserve. Discard skin.

Bring water to boil, add potatoes and salt and cook until potatoes are tender. Drain. With electric mixer whip potatoes and roasted garlic together. Gradually add butter and olive oil. When incorporated, fold in heavy cream and Parmesan cheese. Season with salt and pepper. Serves 6.

Passerelle
Executive Chef Allan J. Vanesko

SAUTEED SNOW PEAS, MUSHROOMS, AND RED AND YELLOW PEPPERS

1 med. yellow pepper, seeded and
    julienned
1 med. red pepper, seeded and
    julienned
1/4 lb. snow peas, strings
    removed

6-8 med. mushrooms, sliced
Salt and pepper to taste
1/4 c. dry white wine

Melt butter in a heavy large skillet over medium-high heat. Add pepper and stir 1 minute. Add mushrooms, saute 2 minutes. Add snow peas and stir about 1 minute. Salt and pepper to taste. Add wine and boil until evaporated, about 1 minute. 2 portions.

O'Flagherty's
Chef Mark Chopko

CREAMED SPINACH

2 pkg. frozen spinach, chopped
1 onion, diced
4 oz. butter
1 c. flour

3 c. warmed milk
Pinch of nutmeg
Salt and pepper to taste

Cook spinach in salted water until done and drain. Saute onion in butter until transparent. Add flour until butter is absorbed. Add hot milk, stir, and cook over medium heat for about 5-10 minutes. Add spinach and season to taste.

Palumbo's Edgmont Inn
Executive Head Chef Richard Hudson

GLAZED CARROTS

4-6 carrots, sliced thin
1 orange
1 lemon
2 whole cloves

1/4 c. burgundy wine
2 tbsp. cornstarch
1/2 c. sugar

Cook carrots until they are al dente (to the bite). Save cooking liquid. Cut in quarter 1 orange and 1 lemon, add cloves, sugar and wine. Mix cornstarch with water until it forms a paste. Add to mixture and cook until clear, about 10 minutes. Strain through fine sieve, add to carrots and serve.

Palumbo's Edgmont Inn
Executive Head Chef Richard Hudson

SHERRIED MUSHROOMS

2 lb. mushrooms
1/4 lb. butter
1/2 gl. chicken broth

1/2 c. cooking sherry
Salt and pepper to taste

Melt butter in medium pot. Add mushrooms and saute until lightly brown. Add chicken broth and sherry, salt and pepper and simmer 8-10 minutes or until tender.

Palumbo's Edgmont Inn
Executive Head Chef Richard Hudson

STRING BEANS AGLIO

1 lb. fresh string beans
3 cloves garlic
5 tbsp. olive oil

Pinch of red pepper
Salt and pepper to taste
2 oz. water

After string beans have been cleaned and cooked, put aside. In a saute pan, put all other ingredients except water. Cook over medium heat until garlic turns golden brown. Add string beans, 2 oz. of water, cover for 2 minutes and serve.

Scampi
Head Chef Ernest Jackson

PAN FRIED POTATOES

2 baked potatoes, chilled, thinly
    sliced
1 green bell pepper, seeded and
    sliced
1/2 med. onion, thinly sliced

8 tbsp. olive oil
Salt and pepper
Fresh chopped cilantro
2 saute pans

In both saute pans, heat 4 tablespoons olive oil each until oil begins to smoke. Lay potatoes in pan so they lay flat. Brown to a crisp on both sides.

In second pan, saute all other ingredients until soft. Combine both in one pan. Mix together, cook 5 minutes more and serve.

Scampi
Head Chef/Proprietor Joseph P. Kirkwood

BAKED ACORN SQUASH WITH BRANDY – BROWN SUGAR BUTTER

3 acorn squash, halved and
    seeded
1/4 lb. softened butter
1 tbsp. brandy

1/4 c. brown sugar
1/4 tsp. cinnamon
2 tbsp. melted butter

Preheat oven to 350 degrees. Drizzle melted butter and cinnamon over squash and bake 45 minutes. Blend together softened butter, brandy and brown sugar. Top cooked squash with brandy butter mixture.

Dugal's Inn
Chef Geoff Young

GLAZED MINI CARROTS AND SHALLOTS

1/2 lb. baby carrots, peeled
4 lg. shallots, peeled
1 1/2 tbsp. butter

1 tbsp. water
1 tbsp. brown sugar
Chopped parsley

Blanch carrots and shallots in a pot of boiling water for 1 minute. Drain. Transfer to a bowl of ice water and cool.

Melt butter with sugar and water in a heavy large saucepan over medium heat. Add vegetables and toss to coat. Season with salt and pepper. Cover. Cook until vegetables are tender. Stir occasionally, about 20 minutes. Top with parsley. 2 portions.

O'Flagherty's
Chef Mark Chopko

SWEET POTATO AND CARROT PUREE'

2 lb. fresh sweet potatoes
1 lb. peeled carrots
1 c. Creme Fraiche'
1/2 c. sour cream
1/2 c. heavy cream
1/4 c. granulated sugar

6 oz. lightly salted butter, room softened
1 tbsp. salt
1/2 tsp. nutmeg
1/4 tsp. cayenne

Make Creme Fraiche' 24 hours in advance.

Mix sour cream and heavy cream in bowl. Cover and set at room temperature. Place sweet potatoes on sheet pan and bake at 375 degrees until skin is wrinkled and potato is cooked. While potatoes are cooking, peel carrots and cut 1/4 inch dice. Place in saucepan with 1 cup of water and cook covered with granulated sugar and salt. Cook until soft.

When carrots are done and potatoes are done, peel skin off potatoes and combine with carrots in food processor. Add remaining ingredients until soft and fluffy. Heat in a dish at 325 degrees until lightly browned on top. Serve with any poultry dish. Serves 6.

Septembers Place
Banquet Chef John Marco

ONCE-BAKED, PAN-FRIED POTATO CAKES

6 cooled baked potatoes, peeled and grated
6 lg. mushrooms, sliced sm.
2 scallions, sliced sm.
1 tbsp. crushed fresh garlic
1 tbsp. chopped fresh basil
1 tbsp. chopped parsley
1/2 c. grated Parmesan cheese
2 eggs
Salt and pepper to taste

Mix all ingredients thoroughly. Pat into 4 oz. patties. Flour both sides and cook in drawn butter over medium heat until browned on both sides. Add salt and pepper to taste. Makes 6-8 servings.

The Gas Light
Head Chef Mark Van Horn

SOUTHWESTERN VEGETABLES

1/2 c. fresh sweet corn
8 asparagus spears, steamed al dente, cut into 1/4 inch pieces
1 lg. red pepper, 1/4 inch dice
1 lg. green pepper, 1/4 inch dice
1 lg. scallion, sliced thin
6 oz. drawn butter
Pinch of salt
Pinch of garlic salt
Pinch of white pepper
Pinch of cayenne pepper
Pinch of thyme
Pinch of chili powder
1/2 tsp. cilantro
5 tbsp. whole butter

Heat drawn butter on high heat. Add vegetables and toss for 2 minutes. Add spices and toss for 1 minute. Add whole butter, toss, and serve. Makes 6-8 servings.

The Gas Light
Head Chef Mark Van Horn

EXTRA RECIPES

POTPOURRI

GARLIC

POTPOURRI

To determine whether an egg is fresh without breaking the shell, immerse the egg in a pan of cool salted water. If it sinks to the bottom, it is fresh. If it rises to the surface, throw it away.

Vinegar brought to a boil in a new frying pan will prevent food from sticking.

When frying, turn a metal colander upside down over the skillet. This allows steam to escape, but keeps the fat from spattering.

Club soda cleans and polishes kitchen appliances at the same time.

When a drain is clogged with grease, pour a cup of salt and a cup of baking soda into the drain followed by a kettle of boiling water. The grease will usually dissolve immediately and open the drain.

Rub stainless steel sinks with lighter fluid if rust marks appear. After the rust disappears, wipe with your regular kitchen cleaner.

Once an onion has been cut in half, rub the left-over side with butter and it will keep fresh longer.

Popcorn: It should always be kept in the freezer. Not only will it stay fresh, but freezing helps eliminate "old maids." "Old Maids" can also be eliminated by running ice cold water over the kernels before throwing into the popper.

Pinch of rosemary to water cooking rice will add an interesting flavor.

Cook wild meats with onions, cuts down wild flavor.

Do you substitute ingredients? This is always risky - don't do it! For example, sifted flour is not interchangeable with unsifted.

Food will keep hot up to 1 hour if taken somewhere, by wrapping hot food in double thickness of aluminum foil.

Garlic helps to prevent cholesterol build up. Helps prevent heart disease by slashing cholesterol levels in the blood and lowering dangerous blood fat levels.

Don't let spilled wine spoil your prettiest tablecloth. While the stain is still wet, cover it with a mound of ordinary table salt; when dry just brush away. The salt will absorb the wine so completely you won't even have to wash the cloth.

Shaving cream is one of the most useful upholstery cleaners.

To remove water rings and stains from inside small glass or crystal vases, dampen the inside and add any toilet bowl cleaner. Let stand 10 minutes. Rinse thoroughly.

To clean and shine copper pots, rub with Worcestershire sauce or catsup. The tarnish will disappear.

To get cotton white socks white again, boil in water to which a slice of lemon has been added.

BANANA PANCAKES

Bananas, diced   Pancake mix for 10-12 pancakes

SAUCE:

1/2 c. butter   2 sliced bananas
1/2 c. brown sugar   1/2 c. maple syrup

Follow instructions for 10-12 pancakes. Add 1 medium size diced banana, cook pancakes. Heat butter. Saute banana slices. Add brown sugar and maple syrup. Simmer. Serve over pancakes. Simple to make but you will get raves.

Thyme Catering
Christine Amarosa Neugebauer, C.W.C.

SPINACH TOMATO POLENTA

2 qt. chicken stock   1/4 oz. fresh chopped garlic
3 c. cornmeal   1 lb. mushrooms, any kind
1 tbsp. salt   1/4 lb. butter
2 oz. butter   2 oz. heavy cream
1/2 c. olive oil   2 lb. spinach
5 oz. tomato paste   Oil
1 oz. basil   1 c. grated Parmesan cheese

Heat olive oil, lightly saute garlic, basil and chopped spinach. Add tomato paste to cook out the acid. Add chicken stock, bring to a boil. Gradually add cornmeal in a steady stream. Whisk until smooth, should NOT have lumps. Then stir the bottom so polenta doesn't stick and burn. Cook on medium-low heat 45 minutes.

Swirl in the 2 oz. of butter. Add salt as needed. Smooth out onto sheet pans lined with plastic. Let cool and set. Brown top under broiler after sprinkling with Parmesan cheese. Cut into desired shapes. Saute mushrooms, add cream and seasoning and reduce. Serve over polenta.

Thyme Catering
Christine Amarosa Neugebauer, C.W.C.

PACKY'S ROSE' SAUCE

1 oz. clarified butter
1/4 tsp. oregano
1/4 tsp. basil
1/4 tsp. fresh chopped garlic
1/2 oz. tarragon vinegar
2 oz. white wine

4 oz. heavy cream
2 oz. your favorite marinara
  sauce
1 oz. freshly grated Romano
  cheese

Saute garlic in butter until smell breaks from pan. Then add oregano and basil and deglaze with white wine and tarragon vinegar. Reduce to half, add heavy cream, reduce to half again. Then add marinara and cheese. Simmer to thick consistency for ravioli or leave looser for spaghetti or linguini.

Packy's Pub
Head Chef Matthew Thompson

MARINARA SAUCE

1 (#5) can whole tomato in
  juice, crushed
1 sm. Spanish onion, diced
3 sm. cloves garlic, minced
1/2 c. fresh parsley, chopped

1/2 c. pure virgin olive oil
Pinch of red pepper seed
Pinch of oregano
1 tsp. salt

Simmer onion, garlic, and parsley in a saucepan with oil. When the onion becomes translucent, add seasoning and crushed tomatoes. Cook for 1/2 hour on low heat.

Towne Crier Inn
Chef/Proprietor David Iannucci

PESTO SAUCE

1 bunch fresh basil leaves
5 cloves garlic
1/2 c. pine nuts

1/4 c. Parmesan cheese
1/4 c. olive oil

In food processor, chop garlic and pine nuts. Add basil and Parmesan cheese and blend. Slowly drizzle olive oil into mixture until desired consistency is achieved.

For a topping, make into a thick paste. For a pasta sauce, add oil to a thinner consistency.

Dugal's Inn
Head Chef Scott Nyman

DUGAL'S SHRIMP BAKE

4 Idaho potatoes
4 jumbo shrimp, peeled and
   deveined

4 slices bacon
1 1/2 tbsp. horseradish

LAMAZE:

1/4 c. Russian dressing
1/4 c. sour cream

1 tbsp. horseradish

Bake potatoes at 350 degrees for 1 hour. Stuff each shrimp with 1/4 tablespoon of horseradish and wrap with bacon. Cook 25 minutes at 350 degrees or until golden brown. Mix final 3 ingredients together for Lamaze dressing. When potato and shrimp are cooked, split open potato. Top with cooked shrimp, then top with Lamaze sauce. Serves 4.

Dugal's Inn
Chef Geoff Young

WHITE PIZZA

DOUGH:

1 tsp. active yeast (1/2 pkg.)
1 tsp. sugar
1 c. warm water (105 to 115
   degrees)

2 1/2 c. all-purpose flour
1 tsp. salt

Stir the yeast and sugar into the water in a small bowl and let the mixture stand 10 minutes or until foamy. Using a food processor, put flour and salt in the work bowl and turn machine on. With machine running, pour in yeast mixture. Process the dough 40 seconds. Transfer to a oiled bowl and rotate to coat the dough with oil. Cover with a damp towel and place in a warm place for 1 hour or until doubled in bulk.

4 tbsp. pesto sauce (available at specialty shops)
8 oz. Mozzarella, shredded
4 oz. ricotta cheese

2 tbsp. sun-dried tomatoes, chopped
10-12 lg. spinach leaves, cleaned, picked, coarsely chopped

Preheat oven to 450 degrees. Roll the dough into a 15-inch round on a floured board. If it refuses to stretch, let it rest a few minutes and try again. Put the dough on a 16-inch oiled pizza pan. Smear pesto evenly on top of dough. Add spinach, Mozzarella and dot with ricotta evenly, then sprinkle with sun-dried tomatoes. Place in oven 15-18 minutes or until bottom is lightly brown. Cut in 8 sections and serve.

O'Flagherty's
Chef Mark Chopko

HORSERADISH, GREEN PEPPERCORN CREAM SAUCE

1/2 c. horseradish
1/2 c. green peppercorns
1 qt. heavy cream

2 shallots, peeled and chopped
1 c. cognac
1 tbsp. butter

In saucepan, melt butter over low heat. Add shallots and green peppercorns. Cook for 1 minute. Deglaze with cognac. Reduce halfway, add cream and bring to rolling boil. Reduce to desired thickness, combine horseradish and serve. Can be used with fish or beef as a flavorful sauce.

Bobby's Seafood Restaurant
Sous Chef Norman Whitefield

CREAMY HERB DRESSING

1 qt. mayonnaise
2 1/2 c. heavy cream
1 c. vinegar
1 c. sour cream
3 tbsp. chopped garlic
1 c. finely chopped onion
1/2 tsp. Tabasco

1/2 tsp. Worcestershire
1 tsp. black pepper
1/4 c. fresh chopped oregano
1/4 c. fresh chopped basil
1/4 c. fresh chopped rosemary
1 tsp. fresh thyme
1/4 c. fresh dill

Slowly add first 4 ingredients into mixer. Blend well. Add remaining ingredients with mixer running at slow speed until desired consistency. A blend of fresh herbs in a rich creamy dressing.

Bobby's Seafood Restaurant
Executive Chef Bob Donovan

ROASTED GARLIC, LEMON, BASIL, OLIVE OIL

1 whole clove garlic
1 qt. extra virgin olive oil
1 bunch fresh basil, cut julienne
3 whole lemons

2 qt. glass bottle for storage and cork
1 tsp. cracked black pepper

Rub whole garlic clove with olive oil. Place on a small sheet pan covering with foil and roast for 25 minutes. Let cool. Peel skin off of individual cloves. Put to side. Fill bottle with olive oil. Cut 2 lemons and squeeze juice through top of bottle. Take remaining lemon and peel skin, cut into strips and put into bottle. Squeeze juice of peeled lemon to bottle. Add basil leaves and black pepper. Take peeled garlic cloves, smash each clove lightly with knife and add to bottle. Cork tightly and let sit for a minimum of 12 hours. Shake well before using. A tasty oil to complement salads, pasta or fish.

Bobby's Seafood Restaurant
Executive Chef Bob Donovan

EXTRA RECIPES

Contributors

EXTRA RECIPES

INDEX

MARY'S POACHED PEAR AND CHOCOLATE 44
PEACHES AND CREAM PIE 42
PECAN CARAMEL SAUCE FOR CHOCOLATE
BREAD PUDDING 43
PECAN PIE 35
PISTACHIO ICE CREAM 36
POMPEI'S FAMOUS CHEESECAKE 36
RASPBERRY, PISTACHIO AND MILK CHOCOLATE
BON BONS 39
RIPE BANANA CREME CARAMEL 37
VANILLA CINNAMON TOASTED ALMOND ICE
CREAM 35
WHITE CHOCOLATE MOUSSE 33

Main Dishes

ALL JUMBO LUMP CRAB CAKES 53
BAKED ROUGHY, GENEVA STYLE 69
BAKED SEA BASS BONA-VISTA 86
BAKED STUFFED SPARERIBS 111
BAYOU COMBO 110
BEEF AND PEPPER STEAK 91
BLACK ANGUS SIRLOIN STEAK WITH MUSHROOM
DUXELLE AND BRIE CHEESE 106
BLACK DIAMOND STRIP 109
BLACKENED DUCK BREAST ASPARAGUS SALAD
WITH RASPBERRY VINAIGRETTE 104
BONELESS CHICKEN BREAST IN RASPBERRY
MARINADE 70
BREADED VENISON CHOPS 76
BROILED MARINATED STEAK 60
BROWNED PORK CHOPS 58
CAJUN PAN FRIED CRAB CAKES 101
CAJUN PRIMAVERA 56
CHAR-GRILLED NEW YORK STRIP STEAK WITH
ROASTED RED PEPPERS AND BRIE 94
CHICKEN ALA KING 90
CHICKEN ALA ORANGE 85
CHICKEN AND DUMPLINGS 115
CHICKEN AND FENNEL RISOTTO 71
CHICKEN BREAST WITH OLIVES, ROASTED PEP-
PERS & FETA CHEESE 67
CHICKEN CHASSEUR 112
CHICKEN DE PECHE' 102
CHICKEN DIJONNAISE 77
CHICKEN DIVAN WITH MUSHROOM SAUCE 92
CHICKEN EL PASO 108
CHICKEN FLORENTINE 50
CHICKEN FLORENTINE 113
CHICKEN FRANCAISE 77
CHICKEN HUNTER STYLE 80

CHICKEN MARABELLA 102
CHICKEN NOLA 75
CHICKEN POT PIE 113
CHICKEN RADIATORE 78
CHICKEN ROCKEFELLER 110
CHICKEN SCALLOPINI ALLA MARSALA 62
CHICKEN SONOMA 94
CHICKEN TERESA 84
CHICKEN WITH CAPERS AND OLIVES 59
CHICKEN, BROCCOLI AND TOMATO OVER CAP-
PELLINI 115
CORNISH HENS WITH ROSEMARY WINE SAUCE 61
CRAB CAKES 113
CRAB CAKES WITH PECAN SAUCE 51
CRAB DE NANGREDE 74
CRAB IMPERIAL 83
CRAB STUFFED CHICKEN 83
CRANBERRY GLAZED SPARERIBS 60
CRAWFISH ETOUFFEE 75
CREAM CRAB AU GRATIN 90
DEBRA'S ROAST LEG OF LAMB 76
DOC LOBSTER 54
DUCK CONFIT QUESADILLA 73
FENNEL-GLAZED PORK LOIN 61
FETTUCCINE WITH CHICK PEAS AND BASIL 61
FETTUCCINE WITH CHICKEN AND SWEET PEP-
PERS 63
FILET AND SHRIMP WITH CAPELLINI 65
FILET MIGNON TORNADOE WITH ROASTED PEP-
PER, GREEN PEPPERCORN AND MUST 87
FILET WITH STOUDT 89
FISH STEAKS WITH ROSEMARY 57
FLOUNDER STUFFED WITH SUN-DRIED
TOMATOES, FETA, SPINACH, AND PINE NU 97
FROG LEGS PROVENCALE 111
GOLDEN TROUT WITH HAZELNUTS 64
GREEN EGGS AND HAM 55
GRILLED BREAST OF CHICKEN WITH RASPBERRY
VINAIGRETTE 100
GRILLED CHICKEN WITH LEEKS AND SMOKED
BACON OVER RICE 79
GRILLED LAMB CHOP AND FETA SALAD WITH
BALSAMIC VINAIGRETTE 103
GRILLED SALISBURY STEAK 91
GRILLED SIRLOIN WITH ROASTED CORN AND
TOMATO SALSA 71
GRILLED VEAL CHOPS, SAGE AND MARSALA
SAUCE 63
GRILLED VENISON TENDERLOIN 101

Potpourri

Soups and Salads

Vegetables

Lunch, Dinner
Sunday Brunch

American Bistro

Village Mall, Second Floor
Route 420
Morton, PA 19070
543-3033

RESTAURANT & GRILL

James E. Webb
Guy Angelo Sileo

Private Parties

SEAFOOD
Bobby's
RESTAURANT

Captain
Bobby Keough
Proprietor

5492 West Chester Pike • Newtown Square, PA 19073 •610/296-4430
FAX 610/296-4689

---

(610) 521-9846
(610) 521-9491

HOME MADE
ITALIAN CUISINE

Rossi's
Town Inn
RESTAURANT & BAR

"Philadelphia Dining Comes to Delaware County"

George Rossi
Proprietor

414 Powhattan Ave.
Essington, PA 19029

ELANA'S
414 South 2nd Street
Fine Italian Cuisine
215-574-1687

Open 7 Days
Serving from 5:00 p.m.

---

(215) 627-2590

Proprietors:
Judy DeVicaris
Bill Curry

NOLA CAFÉ

328 SOUTH STREET • PHILADELPHIA, PA 19147

The Jewel of Chester County

Dugal's Inn

fine dining in a
country home atmosphere

Box 770 Rd #4
Strasburg Road
Mortonville PA 19320

Reservations Requested
486-0953

Linda & Scott Nyman
Proprietors

Fireside
Banquets • Family Style Restaurant

61 Baltimore Pike
Springfield, Del Co., PA. 19064
(610) 544-3830

Frank Cacciutti
Proprietor

Kathryn's Inn

Mon. To Thurs.
4 pm to 10pm
Fri. & Sat.
4 pm to 11 pm
Sun 3 pm to 9 pm
Lunch Mon to Sat.
11 am to 3 pm

Banquet Restaurant and Entertainment Center
Drexeline Shopping Center
4990 State Road, Drexel Hill, PA 19026
623-6900

Bobby's Bucks $5

$5.00 $5.00

Good for $5.00 off 2 Dinners Sunday thru Thursday. Not to be combined with any other offer or Discount. **Void on Holidays**

$5.00 $5.00

CAFE ELANA
$10.00 OFF*

2 Dinners, Sunday thru Thursday

* Not to be combined with any other offer, discount, special, All you can eat or Transmedia. Void on Holidays

With This Coupon

$10.00 OFF*

2 Dinners, Sunday thru Thursday

* Not to be combined with any other offer, discount, special, All you can eat or Transmedia. Void on Holidays

With This Coupon

$10.00 OFF*

2 Dinners, Sunday thru Thursday

* Not to be combined with any other offer, discount, special, All you can eat or Transmedia. Void on Holidays

With This Coupon

$10.00 OFF*

2 Dinners, Sunday thru Thursday

* Not to be combined with any other offer, discount, special, All you can eat or Transmedia. Void on Holidays

With This Coupon

$5.00 OFF*

2 Dinners, Sunday thru Thursday

* Not to be combined with any other offer, discount, special, All you can eat or Transmedia. Void on Holidays

With This Coupon

$10.00 OFF*

2 Dinners, Sunday thru Thursday

* Not to be combined with any other offer, discount, special, All you can eat or Transmedia. Void on Holidays

With This Coupon

FREE DINNER*
Sun. Thru Thursday

*Buy one Dinner from the **Regular** Menu and get the second of equal or lesser value FREE! Not to be combined with any other offer, discount special, All you can eat, or Transmedia.

With This Coupon

THE LAGOON

HOTEL
RESTAURANT & NIGHTCLUB

Restaurant open 7 days
From 11 am to 11 pm
Sports Bar Mon. & Tues.
11 am to 11 pm
Night Club Tues. to Sun.
11 am to 2 am
Hotel Open 24 Hours
7 Days a Week

101 Taylor Avenue
Essington, PA 19029

Rest: (610)521-3636
Hotel: (610) 521-1400
Fax: (610) 521-4642

Casual
Elegance
for your
pleasure.

Take
Out
Available

Open 7 Days
11 am to 2 am

3333 Pennell Road (Rt. 452), Media, PA

Fax (610) 558-2066

(610) 558-1929

Lunch & Dinner

PACKY'S PUB

Charlie Mayer Jr.
General Manager

113 W. State Street
Media, PA 19063
(610) 891-0810
Fax (610) 891-6679

Palumbo's EDGMONT INN

Lunch   Dinner   Weddings   Private Parties

Providence Road & West Chester Pike
Edgmont, PA. 19028

356-6310
356-9859

Robert Kellock
Chef

(215) 646-2885

Pike Family Restaurant

Since 1951

820 N. Bethlehem Pike • Box 242 • Spring House, PA 19477

Lunches - Dinners - Banquet Facilities - Cocktail Lounge
Music & Dancing - Friday & Saturday

Riddle Ale House   Pompei's

Famous for Beef, Seafood and Cocktails

ARNOLD J. POMPEI
LO 6-9984 or LO 6-6212

BALTIMORE PIKE
MEDIA, PA. 19063

Rosario's
RESTAURANT
— & —
TAVERN

Route 420 & Morton Ave.
Morton, PA 19070

(610) 544-2744

Robert and Patricia
Rottensteiner
Proprietors

Rose Tree Inn

1243 PROVIDENCE RD. • ROSE TREE, MEDIA, PA 19063 • 610-891-1205

$5.00 OFF*

2 Dinners, Sunday thru Thursday

* Not to be combined with any
  other offer, discount, special,
  All you can eat or Transmedia,
  Void on Holidays

With This Coupon

$10.00 OFF*

2 Dinners, Sunday thru Thursday

* Not to be combined with any
  other offer, discount, special,
  All you can eat or Transmedia,
  Void on Holidays

With This Coupon

FREE DINNER*

Value up to $10.00

Sun - Thru Thurs.
*Buy one Dinner from the Regular
Menu and get the second of equal or
lesser value FREE! Not to be combined with any other offer, discount,
special, All you can eat or Transmedia,
Void on Holidays

With This Coupon

FREE LUNCH* OR DINNER Everyday

*Buy one Dinner or Lunch and get
second of equal or Lesser value FREE!
Not to be combined with any other
offer, discount, All you can eat,
Specials, or Transmedia, Void on Holidays

With This Coupon

$10.00 OFF*

2 Dinners, Sunday thru Thursday

* Not to be combined with any other
offer, discount, special, All you can
eat or Transmedia. Void on Holidays

With This Coupon

$5.00 OFF*

2 Dinners, Sunday thru Thursday

* Not to be combined with any
  other offer, discount, special,
  All you can eat or Transmedia,
  Void on Holidays

With This Coupon

$10.00 OFF*

2 Dinners, Sunday thru Thursday

* Not to be combined with any other
offer, discount, special, All you can
eat or Transmedia. Void on Holidays

With This Coupon

FREE Selected APPETIZER!*

Mon. Thru Thurs. at the bar 7 pm - 10 pm

* Not to be combined with any
  other offer, discount, special,
  All you can eat or Transmedia,
  Void on Holidays

With This Coupon

Scampi Ristorante Italiano

Open For Dinner
Tuesday thru Sunday

Famous for Pasta,
Seafood & Steaks

"THE TALK OF THE TOWN"

2312 Garrett Rd., Drexel Hill
284-3333

Scampi Ristorante Italiano

Open for Dinner
Tuesday thru Sunday

Famous for Pasta,
Seafood & Steaks

"THE TALK OF THE TOWN"

2312 Garrett Rd., Drexel Hill
284-3333

September's PLACE

Lunch Mon. thru Sat.
11 am to 3 pm
Dinner Sun. thru Thurs
4 pm to 10pm
Fri. & Sat. 4 pm to 11 pm
Sunday Brunch
10am to 2 pm
Snacks until Midnight

RESTAURANT
BANQUETS

BRIDAL SALON
ENTERTAINMENT

642 Baltimore Pike, Springfield, PA 19064
544-1230

Seven Stars Inn EST. 1736

7 miles west of Phoenixville
Route 23 & Hoffecker Rd.

(610) 495-5205

(610 566-3338
(610) 566-3309

Thyme Catering
Complete Party Planning
Customized Menus

Jan Cohen
Owner

119 Gayley St.
Media, PA 19063

Iannucci's
**TOWNE
CRIER
INN**

Open
Tues. to Thurs.
5 pm to 10 pm
Fri. & Sat.
5 pm. to 11 pm.
Sundays
4 pm. to 9 pm.

7049 Terminal Square
Upper Darby, Pa.
Phone: 352-1777
Fax: 352-1867

TYMES SQUARE
CLUB MANHATTAN
Restaurant and Banquets

Lunch Mon thru Sat
11 am to 3 pm
Dinner Fri & Sat
4 pm to 11 pm
Sunday 7 pm to 9 pm

2107 MacDade Blvd. Holmes, Pennsylvania 19043
610/586-2900

RESTAURANT
WITH BAR
SINCE 1967

The Gas Light

100 E. HINCKLEY AVE.
RIDLEY PARK, PA 19078
521-4461
OFFICE: 521-9060

DAVID P. LOBB, PROP.

$10.00 OFF*

2 Dinners, Sunday thru Thursday

* Not to be combined with any
other offer, discount, special,
All you can eat, Transmedia, or
$5.00 Pasta night, Void on Holidays

With This Coupon

$10.00 OFF*

2 Dinners, Sunday thru Thursday

* Not to be combined with any
other offer, discount, special,
All you can eat, Transmedia, or
$5.00 Pasta night, Void on Holidays

With This Coupon

$10.00 Gift Certificate

Towards purchase of 2 Dinners,
Sunday thru Thursday at the
7 Stars Inn

$10.00 OFF*

2 Dinners, Sunday thru Thursday

* Not to be combined with any other
offer, discount, special, All you can
eat or Transmedia. Void on Holidays

With This Coupon

$10.00 OFF*

2 Dinners, Sunday thru Thursday

* Not to be combined with any other
offer, discount, special, All you can
eat or Transmedia. Void on Holidays

With This Coupon

10% OFF any banquet or party

For over 50 guests
at your location

With This Coupon

FREE DINNER*

Up To A
$10.00
Value

Sunday thru Thursday
*Buy one Dinner from the regular menu
and get the second of equal or lesser
value FREE! Not to be combined
with any other offer, discount,
or Transmedia. Void on Holidays

With This Coupon

$10.00 OFF*

2 Dinners, Sunday thru Thursday

* Not to be combined with any other
offer, discount, special, All you can
eat or Transmedia. Void on Holidays

With This Coupon

175 *King of Prussia Road, Radnor, PA* 215/293-9521

Open 7 Days a Week
Mon. - Sat. 11:30 am - 2 am
Sunday Brunch 10:30 am - 2:30 pm
Sunday Dinner 5 pm - 10 pm
DJ/Entertainment

39 Morris Ave. □ Bryn Mawr, PA 19010 □ (215) ☎ C-E-N-T-R-A-L

Restaurant Passerelle

For lunch & dinner, business & pleasure,
banquets & superb private dining.

175 King of Prussia Road Radnor, PA 19087
(Exit 5 on Route 476) 215-293-9411 FAX: 293-0161

JOHN AND ANTHONY POLSELLI   (610) LE 4-8191

Trieste Restaurant

SPECIALIZING IN ITALIAN FOOD
COCKTAILS

WHY COOK - CALL US

641 CHESTER PIKE
PROSPECT PARK, PA.

RESTAURANT

210

⊠
THE RITTENHOUSE
Condominium Residences and Hotel

Jim Coleman
Executive Chef
Thomas J. Harkins
Sous Chef

210 West Rittenhouse Square
Philadelphia, Pennsylvania 19103

Direct Dial: 215-790-2509
Hotel: 215-546-9000

TREE TOPS

⊠
The Rittenhouse
Condominium Residences and Hotel
Jim Coleman
Executive Chef
Guillermo A. Pernot
TreeTops Chef De Cuisine

210 West Rittenhouse Square
Philadelphia, Pennsylvania 19103

Direct Dial: 215 - 790-2509
Hotel 215-546-9000

Three Styles - One Fine Quality

B I S T R O

A PLACE FOR A FEAST

281 MONTGOMERY AVE.
BALA CYNWYD, PA 19004
TEL (610) 667-1245
FAX (610) 667-7239
Middle Eastern, American
Eatery & Bar

EVVIVA

Fine Dining & Parties

1236 Montgomery Ave.
Narberth, PA 19072
Tel (610) 667-1900

Dining & Catering
© copyright Wakim Brothers

Marbles

Restaurant & Bar

818 Lancaster Ave.
Bryn Mawr, PA 19010
Tel (610) 520-9100
Fax (610) 520-9221

Casual Dining

PROPRIETORS THE KURTZHALZ FAMILY

The Ingleneuk
Tea House
& CATERING
SINCE 1916

DINNER
WED.-SAT.
5:30pm-8pm
SUNDAY
1pm-6pm

LUNCH
WED.-SAT.
11:30am-2pm

120 Park Av.e
Swarthmore. Pa. 19081

(610) 543-4569

Order additional copies of our group's cookbook. Use the handy order form below:

Please send me _____ copies of your cookbook @ $14.95 each, plus $2.00 postage and handling per book ordered. Mail your order to:

Please Send me
Head Chefs
Recipes
Vol 1 ☐

The Independent Restaurant Association
1 East Park Avenue
Havertown, PA 19083

Please send me
Head Chefs
Recipes
Vol II ☐

Mail Books To:

Name:_____

Address:_____

City,State,Zip:_____

For Further Information Contact:
The Independent Restaurant Association
1 East Park Ave.
Havertown, PA 19083

Order additional copies of our group's cookbook. Use the handy order form below:

Please send me _____ copies of your cookbook @ $14.95 each, plus $2.00 postage and handling per book ordered. Mail your order to:

Please Send me
Head Chefs
Recipes
Vol 1 ☐

The Independent Restaurant Association
1 East Park Avenue
Havertown, PA 19083

Please send me
Head Chefs
Recipes
Vol II ☐

Mail Books To:

Name:_____

Address:_____

City,State,Zip:_____

For Further Information Contact:
The Independent Restaurant Association
1 East Park Ave.
Havertown, PA 19083

A Collection Of Helpful Hints And Useful Information.

HOW TO SET A TABLE

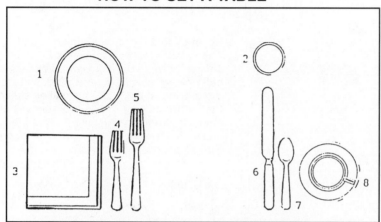

Table set-up for a simple meal.

1.) Bread and butter plate
2.) Water glass
3.) Napkin
4.) Salad fork
5.) Dinner fork
6.) Knife
7.) Teaspoon
8.) Coffee cup.

Place the silver about 1 inch from the edge of the table. Place knives, forks, and spoons in the order of their use. Knives are placed at the right of the plate, with the cutting edge turned inward. Place the spoons, bowls up, at the right of the knives. Place the forks, tines up, at the left of the plate.

BASIC RULES FOR SERVING YOUR GUESTS

*   All food is served from the left.

*   All beverages are served from the right.

*   Serve women, older persons, and children first; in a group of women or men, begin with the person to the right of the host and proceed counterclockwise.

*   Clear dishes from the right.

*   Do not stack or scrape dishes before a guest.

1

NCS® M99491:321

Printed in U.S.A.

HINTS hints HINTS hints HINTS hints HINTS hints HINTS hints HINTS hints HINTS hints HINTS hints HINTS hints HINTS hints HINTS hints HINTS HINTS

ADD ELEGANCE TO A TABLE SETTING
CHARM YOUR GUESTS WITH THESE SIMPLE NAPKIN FOLDS

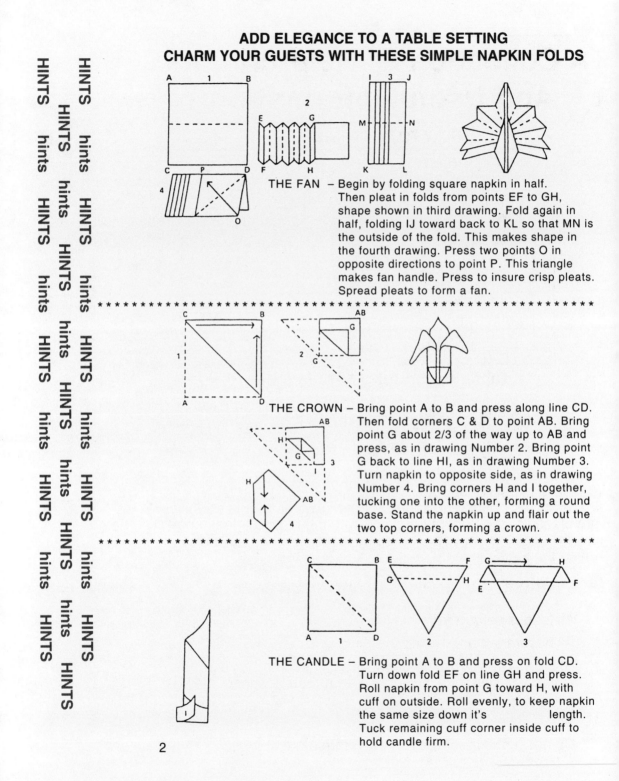

THE FAN – Begin by folding square napkin in half. Then pleat in folds from points EF to GH, shape shown in third drawing. Fold again in half, folding IJ toward back to KL so that MN is the outside of the fold. This makes shape in the fourth drawing. Press two points O in opposite directions to point P. This triangle makes fan handle. Press to insure crisp pleats. Spread pleats to form a fan.

* *

THE CROWN – Bring point A to B and press along line CD. Then fold corners C & D to point AB. Bring point G about 2/3 of the way up to AB and press, as in drawing Number 2. Bring point G back to line HI, as in drawing Number 3. Turn napkin to opposite side, as in drawing Number 4. Bring corners H and I together, tucking one into the other, forming a round base. Stand the napkin up and flair out the two top corners, forming a crown.

* *

THE CANDLE – Bring point A to B and press on fold CD. Turn down fold EF on line GH and press. Roll napkin from point G toward H, with cuff on outside. Roll evenly, to keep napkin the same size down it's   length. Tuck remaining cuff corner inside cuff to hold candle firm.

2

SIMPLE TRICKS — ELEGANT RESULTS

FRUIT BASKETS

To enhance your next dinner party, let this fruit basket charm your guest, and add color to the meal.

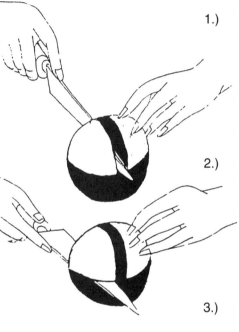

1.) Trim the bottom end of an orange or grapefruit flat. Place fruit upright. Make an imaginary line around the middle of the fruit.

Cut down the right side of the center until you reach the line. Do the left side to the center.

2.) Cut on the horizontal line on the right side of the middle, until you reach the right side vertical cut. repeat on the left side.

3.) Add charm to your fruit basket by scoring the rind, to create a basket weave effect. Remove pulp from fruit.

4.) Fill baskets with fruit.

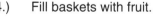

NCS® M99491:321

Printed in U.S.A.

HINTS hints HINTS hints HINTS hints HINTS hints HINTS hints HINTS hints HINTS hints HINTS hints HINTS hints HINTS hints HINTS hints HINTS

3

ONION FLOWER

Before you begin you will need: a small onion, sharp paring knife, ice water, and a skewer.

Steps:
1.) Peel the onion. Hold it so that the onion point is on top.
2.) Make the first cut by taking the knife directly down the middle, using a rocking motion. Do not cut completely through the onion.

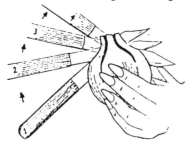

3.) Turn the onion and repeat the step above. Continue this process until there is no more onion to cut.
4.) Place the onion in ice water and the onion will bloom. You may add food color to the ice water to give your flower color.
5.) You may skewer the onion flower at the stem end, or just set on a tray to garnish your food.

RADISH FLOWER

1.) Hold the radish with the stem end down, make four cuts down all the around the radish.
2.) Peel off the top portion or, leave as it is.
3.) Place radish flower in water to bloom.

HINTS HINTS hints hints HINTS hints HINTS hints HINTS hints HINTS hints HINTS hints HINTS hints HINTS hints HINTS hints HINTS hints HINTS hints HINTS HINTS

BREAD MACHINE BAKING TIPS

1.) Review your instructions on how your bread machine operates carefully. Your manual can provide troubleshooting guide should your bread not come out perfect. Never open bread machine during the rising of baking stages to check the breads progress. Opening the bread machine may cause the bread to collapse.

2.) Correctly assemble your bread machine. Make certain the parts are properly put together, so you mix and knead properly.

3.) Read and understand your recipe before you begin. Only use the ingredients listed and measure carefully.

4.) Ingredients should be pre-measured and at room temperature before adding them to the bread machine. Add ingredients listed in proper order as recipe calls for.

5.) If your bread machine has a delayed bake cycle for recipes that do not have dairy or egg products (so bacteria won't grow as the mixture sits in the bread machine.) Do not have yeast come with liquid when using the delayed bake cycle.

TROUBLESHOOTING

* **BREAD DIDN'T RISE -** Rising will decease with too much sugar or fat.

* **BREAD IS TOO BROWN -** Browning too quickly caused by too much sugar or fat.

* **BREAD IS TOO HEAVY -** Too much flour used, not enough liquid, and not enough yeast.

* **BREAD IS UNDERCOOKED -** Too much liquid used in recipe or too much flour used.

* **BREAD HAS A YEASTY AROMA -** OR OVER PROOFED - Decrease the amount of yeast in recipe by 1/4 teaspoon.

USEFUL KITCHEN HINTS

Substitute for sour cream - mix 1 tablespoon lemon juice, 1 cup cottage cheese, 1/3 cup buttermilk. Blend in a blender or food processor for 2 minutes.

One lemon will yield about 2 1/2 and 3 1/2 tablespoons of juice.

To cut dried fruits, marshmallows or gumdrops, dip kitchen scissors frequently into hot water.

A medium-size clove of garlic equals 1/8 teaspoon of garlic powder.

You get twice the amount of orange juice from a orange, if you hold it under hot water before you squeeze.

Popcorn left in the cupboard? Place 1/4 cup of popcorn in a brown paper lunch bag. Fold the top over a few times. Place paper on it's side and microwave on high until the popping slows.

Brew your coffee with bottled spring water, you will have better tasting coffee and no mineral deposits.

NCS® M99491:321

Printed in U.S.A.

MINUS MEAT COOKERY

TOFU – Sometimes called bean curd, is a white or cream- colored product made from soybean milk. Soft tofu is smooth and creamy. Use it for whipping, blending, crumbling for recipes such as dips and dressings. Firm tofu is used for slicing and cubing. Use in stir-frys, casseroles, soups, and any other dish you want the shape to stay intact.

BARLEY – Has a mild, starchy flavor and slightly chewy texture. Use as side dishes hot cereal, soups, and baked goods.

BULGUR – A precooked and dried, cracked wheat with a tan color and a delicious nutty flavor. Serve as a side dish, salad (Tabbouleh).

CORNMEAL – Medium-fine ground, hulled kernels that are MADE from corn kernels. Cornmeal comes in white, yellow, and blue varieties. Stone ground corn meal is slightly coarser than other cornmeal. Use in baked goods, coating, polenta.

MASA HARINA – Is corn processed with lime to remove hull, medium ground; dry, dough, raw, or cooked tortillas. Used in tortillas and other mexican dishes.

MILLET – A tiny round yellow kernels have a slightly nutty flavor and chewy texture when cooked. Use for side dishes and flat breads.

COUSCOUS – Is a tiny pasta made from semolina pellets, often parcooked. Often served as stew and in soups.

QUINOA (kih-no-uh) – Tiny grain is about the size of sesame seeds, is pale yellow and has a crunchy texture and a subtle nutty taste. It's low-fat source of fiber and complete protein.

WILD RICE – Is not a rice but a long, dark brown grass. Wild rice has a nutty flavor and is used as a side dish & in stuffings.

WHITE RICE – Polished grains, usually enriched; long or short grain. Used in puddings, risotto.

BROWN RICE – Hulled grains, bran intact; short, medium, or long grain, may be enriched.

BASMATI RICE – Delicate, extra-long grain, polished. Used as side dishes, pilafs.

CONVERTED RICE – Parcooked, polished grains, may be enriched.

MISO – A salty paste made from cooked, aged soybeans and sometimes grains. Thick and spreadable, it's used for flavoring and soup base. Available in several varieties; darker varieties tend to be stronger-flavored and saltier than lighter varieties.

ARROWROOT POWDER – Starch flour used for thickening. Usually less processed than corn starch, but can substituted for it.

PINE NUTS – Seeds from the pine cones of certain evergreens. Their mild pine-like flavor is enhanced by toasting. Also called, pignolias of pinons. Makes wonderful pesto.

GARBANZO BEANS – Light brown beans with a nutty flavor. Also called chickpeas. Used in Middle Eastern and Mediterranean dishes and salads.

Meatless cookery wouldn't be complete without the various pastas, cheeses, herbs, vegetables, and manyu other ingredients you bring to your recipe.

PASTA

PASTA PASTA

NAME	DESCRIPTION	USE
MACARONI		
Acini di pepe/Peppercorns	Tiny wheat pasta	Soup, salads
Alphabets	Tiny alphabet pasta	Soup
Conchiglie/Shell	Smooth or ridged shell shaped pasta in different sizes	Soup, salads
Elbow Macaroni	Macaroni tubes that are curved	Casseroles, soups
Farfalle/Bow Ties	Bow shaped pasta	Soups, stuffings
Mostaccioli	Diagonally cut pasta	Casseroles, tomato sauces
Orzo	Tiny rice shaped pasta	Cooked like rice, soups
Rigatoni	Ridged curved tubes	Casseroles, soups
Zita	Smooth short tubes	Casseroles
NOODLES		
Fettuccini	Ribbon noodles about 1/2 inch wide	Buttered or in sauce
Lasagna	Wide pasta, with/without curly edges	Baked Casseroles,
Lasagna		
Tagliatelle/Wide Egg Noodle	3/4 inch wide egg noodle	Casseroles
SPAGHETTI		
Capellini/Angel Hair	Thin, sometimes coiled	Sauces
Fusilli/Rotini	Spiral shaped pasta	Casseroles/Sauces
Linuine	Flat, narrow, long	Casseroles, sauces
Vernicelli	Straight thin spaghetti	Sauces
OTHER PASTA		
Manicotto	Large diagonal tubes	cooked and filled
Ravioli	A filled pasta	Serve with sauce

To make homemade pasta follow recipe for ingredients and procedures.

Noodles
1 cup all-purpose flour
1 cup semolina flour
3 egg yolks
1 egg
2 teaspoons salt
1/4 to 1/2 cup water

Methods
Make a well in the center of the four.
All egg yolks and egg, add salt; mix
in thoroughly. Add water, a small amount
at a time, until the dough is stiff but
pliable. Divide the dough in 4 parts
Deep dough covered tightly (so it doesn't dry out), with a
rolling pin or a floured surface, roll dough into a thin
rectangle. Fold rectangle in thirds, cut cross wise into thin
strips. Let noodles air dry until stiff Cook noodles in boiling
salted water until tender, about 6 minutes.

Equipment needed for pasta making:
Collander - Large strainer to drain pasta
Electric Mixer - Dough can be mixed by using a dough hook attachment.
Food Processor - Like the electric mixer, it will mix the dough for you and most of the kneading.
Knife - A sharp long Knife.
Past Wheel/Pastry Wheel - Use cutters to make rows of ravioli and lasagna.
Pasta Machine - Electric or Hand crank models will make uniform sheets of pasta.
Ravioli Stamp - Ravioli can be made one at a time by processing two sheets of pasta with filling inside, pressing shape out and sealing edges.
Ravioli Tray - Looks like an ice cube tray. Place dough on tray, set filling on indentions, place top sheet of pasta on top, roll over top sheet with rolling pin. Separate ravioli's with wheel or free hand.
Rolling Pin - Use a solid, long rolling pin.

NCS® M99491:321 Printed in U.S.A.

FUN FOOD FOR KIDS

Flavored gelatin wedges - Cut a orange in half, remove the pulp, leaving the white membrane and the rind. Place orange halves in muffin tins (to hold in place). Fill each orange with gelatin . Chill until the gelatin is firm. Heat a knife blade with hot water(wipe dry), slice the orange into wedges. Keep refrigerated until ready to serve.

Yogurt Popsicles - 1 Carton plain yogurt

1 (6oz.) concentrated Unsweetened fruit juice (may add dash of vanilla or honey)
Mix well, freeze in 3 oz. paper cups, using wooden sticks or spoons for handles when partially frozen.

Marshmallow Popcorn Balls - 6 Tablespoons butter

3 cups Miniature Marshmallows
1/2 of a 3 oz. pkg. (3 tbsp) Raspberry Gelatin
3 Quarts of popped unsalted popcorn
In a sauce pan, melt butter, add marshmallows and stir until melted. Mix in dry gelatin. Pour mixture over popcorn, and mix well with buttered hands, and form into balls.

Bunny Salad - Place a canned pear half on a bed of lettuce. Add raisins for the eyes, maraschino cherries for the nose, toothpicks for whiskers, and american cheese for the ears.

Edible Play Dough - Mix 1 jar of peanut butter (18 oz.)

6 tablespoons honey
non-fat dry milk powder (until the correct consistency)
(may add cocoa for a chocolate flavor)
Shape any way you want, decorate.

Breakfast Cereal Toppers - Stir in or top cereal with any of the following: Jelly or jam
applesauce
fresh fruit
raisins, dates
ice cream, frozen yogurt
brown sugar or honey

CAFFE WITH LOVE

ESPRESSO: (s-press-o) - 1 fluid ounce of straight coffee (liquid drawn from 7 grams of coffee). Espresso should never be bitter, bitterness occurs from inferior coffee or incorrect brewing process.

LATTE: (lah-tay) - Espresso with steamed milk (2% prefered) added to 1 - 2 inch from the rim of cup, topped with foam.

CAPPUCCINO: (cop-u-chee-no) - Espresso topped with one part milk and one part foam.

MOCHA: (mo-ka) - Place chocolate syrup in bottom of a cup, add espresso, stir, add steamed milk 1/2 inch from top and garnish with whipped cream.

VIENNESE: (v-en-eese) - Add Cinnamon to the coffee grounds before brewing the espresso. Prepare a latte with espresso shot, garnish with whipped cream and a dash of cinnamon

ESPRESSO MACCHIATO: (ma-key-ah-toe) - Espresso topped with a dollop of foam served in a demitasse.

AMMERICANO: (ah-mare-i-con-o) - Espresso diluted with hot water until it reaches the volume of a normal American cup of coffee.

Coffee once opened must be used in a weeks time, to remain fresh.

The milk you use should be whole, 2%, non-fat, and half and half.

Steaming milk is for Lattes, mochas and hot chocolate. It is foamed for Cappuccinos and Macchiatos.
To foam milk, start with a clean pitcher filled 1/3 with cold milk. Hot milk won't foam. Place steam wand under the surface and fully open the steam valve. As the foam rises, lower pitcher until you have the correct amount of foam.

To steam milk, just immerse the steam wand deeper into the pitcher and heat the milk until the pitcher is almost too hot to hold.

Milk can be steamed twice, but it can be foamed once.

Always make Espresso in a warmed cup.

The coffee beans you buy should be carefully blended and roasted for espresso.

True espresso in made by forcing water heated to around 195 degrees F. with pressure through a finely ground coffee. This makes a concentrated flavorful extract which is the body of coffee.

9

NCS® M99491:321

Printed in U.S.A.

HINTS

MICROWAVE COOKING BASICS

Your microwave not only can be used for popcorn and reheating leftovers, but as for melting butter, melting chocolate, warming syrup, soften ice cream, making fast food, cakes, main dishes, and much more.

Microwaves have browning grills, roasting rack, muffin pans, and other microwave utensils. But, begin with what you have: **Glass**-oven proof glass or ceramic baking dishes are the most used cooking tools. Use glass, china, or pottery if there is no metal trim or signature on the bottom.

Plastic - Use dishwasher-safe plastics, hard plastic trays, mugs, and bowls may be used in microwaves for short periods of time. Foam cups and dishes, and baby bottles are safe for heating, but none of these items should be used for prolonged periods because melting may occur. Use plastic wrap as a covering, but pierce it before taking out of microwave to prevent steam burns.

Paper - Paper cups, plates, towels should be used only for heating or defrosting. Long periods of time may cause paper to burn. Wax paper can be used as a cover during cooking.

Metal - In general metal should not be used in your microwave. Microwaves cannot pass through metal and food will only cook from the top. TV dinner trays, less than 3/4 of and inch deep are allowable because they are shallow enough for the microwave to penetrate and cook food from the top.

Metal skewers are usable when the food is much greater than metal, like a filled kabob. Small pieces of foil can be used for shielding parts which are cooking too quickly.

Straw baskets/wood handled spoons and rubber spatulas can be used in oven for short periods of time.

** **Quantity** -determines cooking time. Small amounts of food or liquid take less cooking time than larger amounts of the same ingredient.

** **Density**- dense heavy foods take longer to microwave than lighter foods because microwaves cannot penetrate as deeply and the food must heat by conduction from the hot outer edges.

** **Starting temperature**-room temperature foods cook faster than food that is refrigerated. And refrigerated food cooks faster than frozen foods.

When in doubt always consult your microwave manual for cooking techniques, equipment to use , reheating, defrosting, and cooking your food.

SIMPLE GUIDE TO WEIGHTS, MEASURES AND METRIC

WEIGHTS AND MEASURES

CAN #	FLUID OZ. VOLUME	CUPS
303, also #1	15.6	2
303, cylinder	19.0	2-1/3
2-1/2	28.5	3-1/2
#5	56.0	7
#10	103.7	12-3/4
1 Gallon	128.0	16

COMMON CONVERSIONS

3 Teaspoons (tsp.)	1 Tablespoon (Tbls.)
48 Teaspoons (tsp.)	1 Cup (c.)
4 Tablespoons (Tbls.)	1/4 Cup (c.)
16 Tablespoons (Tbls.)	1 Cup (c.)
1/4 Cup (c.)	2 Ounces (oz.)
1/2 Cup (c.)	4 Ounces (oz.)
1 Cup (c.)	8 Ounces (oz.)
1 Pint Equals 2 Cups	16 Ounces (oz.)
1 Quart Equals 4 Cups	32 Ounces (oz.)
1 Gallon Equals 16 Cups	128 Ounces (oz.)

METRIC CONVERSION TABLE

To Change	To	Multiply By
Ounce (oz.)	Grams (g)	28
Pounds (lbs.)	Kilograms (kg)	0.45
Fluid ounces	Milleliters (ml)	30
Cups (c.)	Liters (l)	0.24
Quarts (qt.)	Liters (l)	0.95
Gallons (gal.)	Liters (l)	3.8
Temperature (F)	Temperature	5/9 after subtracting 32

Putting Metric Units into Daily Living.
Dash of Salt is about 1 ml.
Quart of Milk is just less than 1 liter.
Paper clip weighs 1 g.
Thickness of a dime is 1 mm.
10 to 15 minute walk is 1 km.
Water freezes at 0 degree Celsius.
Water boils at 100 degree Celsius.
Room temperature is 20 degree C to 25 degree C.

NCS® M99491:321

Printed in U.S.A.

LOW FAT - NO FAT - SOME FAT - GUIDE

FOOD TABLE

Abbreviations used in Table

cal.	calories	poly. fatty acid	polyunsaturated fatty acid
chol.	cholesterol	sat. fatty acid	saturated fatty acid
gm	gram	Tbsp.	tablespoon
mg	milligram	tr	trace
Na	sodium	pkg.	package
oz.	ounce		

Description Food/Portion	Weight (gm)	Fat (gm)	sat. Fatty Acid (gm)	Poly. Fatty Acid	Energy (cal.)	Chol. (mg)	Na (mg)
FROZEN DESSERTS							
Frozen Yogurt (1/2 cup)	113	2.3	1.5		123	9	60
Ice Cream, 10% fat (1/2 cup)	67	7.1	4.5		135	30	58
Ice Milk (1/2 cup)	66	2.8	1.8		92	9	53
Sherbet (1/2 cup)	97	1.9	1.2		135	7	44
CHEESE							
American (1 oz)	28	8.9	5.6		106	27	406
Cheddar, Colby, Parmesan, Swiss (1 oz)	28	9.4	6.0		114	30	176
Cottage Cheese, lowfat 1% (1/2 cup)	113	1.2	0.7		82	5	459
Cream Cheese (1 oz)	28	9.9	6.2		74	31	84
Mozzarella. part skim (1 oz)	28	4.5	2.9		72	16	132
Ricotta, part skim (1 oz)	28	2.2	1.4		39	9	35
FATS and OILS							
Margarine-							
Corn Oil (1 tsp)	5	3.8	0.6	1.5	34	0	44
Diet (2 tsp)	10	3.8	0.6	1.5	33	0	51
Safflower Oil, tub (1 tsp)	5	3.8	0.4	2.1	34	0	51
Soybean, tub (1 tsp)	5	3.8	0.6	1.3	34	0	51
Butter (1 tsp)	5	4.1	2.5	0.2	36	11	41
Oil-							
Canola (1 tsp)	5	4.5	0.3	1.5	40	0	0
Corn (1 tsp)	5	4.5	0.6	2.7	40	0	0
Olive (1 tsp)	5	4.5	0.6	0.4	40	0	0
Safflower (1 tsp)	5	4.5	0.4	3.4	40	0	0
Peanut (1 tsp)	5	4.5	0.8	1.4	40	0	0
BREADS, CEREALS, PASTA							
Bagel, 1	100	2.6			296		360
Bread, White (1 slice)	23	0.9	0.2		63		114
English Muffin (half)	29	0.6			69		185
Graham Crackers (4 squares)	228	2.6	0.6		110		190
Saltine Crackers (10)	28	3.4	0.8		123		312
Cornflakes (1 oz)	28	0.1	0.0		110	0	351
Granola (1 oz)	28	7.7	1.4		138		3
Oatmeal, quick/instant (1 cup)	234	2.4	0.4		145	0	1
Noodles, Chow Mein (1 cup)	45	10.6	2.0		220	5	450
Egg Noodles (1 cup)	160	2.4			200	50	3
Rice, Cooked (1 cup)	205	0.2			223	0	4
Spaghetti (1 cup)	140	0.6	0.0		155		1
FRUITS and VEGETABLES							
Vegetables-are low in fat and saturated fat (1/2 to 1 cup)		0.2	0.0		25	0	
Apple, raw (1)	138	0.5	0.1		81	0	1
Banana, half	57	0.3	0.1		53	0	2
Cantaloupe (1 cup)	160	0.4	0.0		57	0	14
Grapefruit (half)	123	0.1	0.0		37	0	0
Grapes (15)	36	0.1	0.0		23	0	0
Orange (1)	131	0.2	0.0		62	0	0
Strawberries (1 1/4 cup)	186	0.7	0.0		56	0	3
Watermelon (1 1/4 cup)	200	0.9	0.0		63	0	4

12

HINTS HINTS hints HINTS hints HINTS hints HINTS hints HINTS hints HINTS hints HINTS hints HINTS hints HINTS hints HINTS hints HINTS hints HINTS hints HINTS hints HINTS HINTS

CHEESE GUIDE

Cheese	How it looks and tastes	How to serve
American, cheddar	Favorite all-around cheeses. Flavor varies from mild to sharp. Color ranges from natural to yellow-orange; texture firm to crumbly.	In sandwiches, casseroles, souffles, and creamy sauces. With fruit pie or crisp crackers; on a snack or dessert tray with fruit.
Blue, Gorgonzola, Roquefort	Compact. creamy cheeses veined with blue or blue-green mold. Sometimes crumbly. Mild to sharp salty flavor. (Stilton is similar, but like a blue-veined Cheddar.)	Crumble in salads, salad dressings, dips. Delicious with fresh pears or apples for dessert. Blend with butter for steak topper. Spread on crackers or crusty French or Italian bread.
Brick	Medium firm; creamy yellow color, tiny holes. Flavor very mild to medium sharp.	Good for appetizers, sandwiches, or deserts. Great with fresh peaches, cherries, or melons.
Brie *(bree)*	Similar to Camember, but slightly firmer. Distinctive sharp flavor, pronounced odor.	Serve as dessert with fresh fruit. Be sure to eat the thin brown and white crust.
Camembert *(kam'em bear)*	Creamy yellow with thin gray-white crust. When ripe, it softens to the consistency of thick cream. Full, rich, mildly pungent.	Classic dessert cheese-serve at room temperature with fresh peaches, pears, or apples , or with toasted walnuts and crackers.
Cottage	Soft, mild, unripened cheese; large or small curd. May have cream added.	Used in salads, dips, main dishes. Popular with fresh and caned fruits.
Cream	Very mild-flavored soft cheese with buttery texture. Rich and smooth. Available whipped and in flavored spreads.	Adds richness and body to molded and frozen salads, cheesecake, dips, frostings, sandwich spreads. Serve whipped with dessert.
Edam, Gouda	Round, red-coated cheeses; creamy yellow to yellow-orange inside; firm and smooth. Mild nutlike flavor.	Bright hub for dessert or snack tray. Good in sandwiches or crunchy salads, or with crackers. Great with grapes and oranges.
Feta *(sheep's or goats)*	Block, white/salty. Lower in fat than most cow's milk cheese.	Soaking the cheese in cold water and draining removes some of the salt
Havarti *(cream enriched cows)*	Buttery may. May be flavored with dill or caraway.	Good on deli trays, crackers.
Liederkranz, Limburger	Robust flavor and highly aromatic. Soft and smooth when ripe. Liederkranz is milder in flavor and golden yellow in color. Limburger is creamy white.	Spread on pumpernickel, rye, or crackers. Team with apples, pears, and Tokay grapes. Serve as snack with salty pretzels and coffee.
Monterey Jack	Wheel or block, Light yellow. Mild semi-soft to hard (depends on aging).	Mexican dishes or casseroles.
Mozzarella Scamorze	Unripened. Mild-flavored and slightly firm. Creamy white to pale yellow.	Cooking cheese. A "must" for pizza, lasagna; good in toasted sandwiches, hot snacks.
Muenster *(Mun' stir)*	Between Brick and Limburger. Mild to mellow flavor, creamy white. Medium hard, tiny holes.	Use in sandwiches or on snack or dessert tray. Good with fresh sweet cherries and melon wedges.
Neufchatel *(whole or skim cows)*	Block, White, Soft and creamy. Mild slightly tangy.	Use in salads, sandwiches, and desserts.
Parmesan, Romano	Sharp, piquant. very hard cheeses. Come in shakers graded. (Parmesan is also available shredded.) Or grate your own.	Sprinkle on pizza, main dishes, breads, salads soups. Shake over buttered pop corn!
Port du Salut *(por du sa lu')*	Semisoft. smooth and buttery. Mellow to robust flavor between Cheddar and Limburger.	Dessert cheese-delicious with fresh fruit; great with apple pie. Good for snack tray.
Provolone *(pro vo lo' nee)*	Usually smoked, mild to sharp flavor. Hard, compact and flaky. Pear or sausage shaped.	Use in Italian dishes, in sandwiches, on snack and appetizer trays.
Ricotta	Mild, sweet, nutlike. Flavor: soft, moist texture with loose curds.	Salads, lasagna, desserts.
Swiss	Firm, pale yellow cheese, with large round holes. Sweet nutlike flavor.	Good in salads, sauces, as a snack.
Process cheeses	A blend of fresh and aged natural cheeses, pasteurized and packaged. Smooth and creamy; melts easily. May be flavored.	Ideal for cheese sauces, souffles, grilled cheese sandwiches, In casseroles. Handy for the snack tray, too.

13

NCS® M99491:321

Printed in U.S.A.

RECOMMENDED STORAGE PERIODS FOR DRY GOODS

HINTS HINTS hints HINTS hints HINTS hints HINTS hints HINTS hints HINTS hints hints HINTS hints HINTS hints HINTS hints HINTS hints HINTS hints HINTS hints HINTS hints hints HINTS hints HINTS

BAKING MATERIALS

Baking powder	8 to 12 months
Chocolate, baking	6 to 12 months
Chocolate, sweetened	2 years
Cornstarch	2 to 3 years
Yeast, dry	18 months
Baking soda	8 to 12 months

BEVERAGES

Coffee, ground, vacuum packed	7 to 12 months
Coffee, ground, not vacuum packed	2 weeks
Coffee, instant	8 to 12 months
Tea, leaves	12 to 18 months
Tea, instant	8 to 12 months
Carbonated beverages	Indefinitely

CANNED FOOD

Fruits, acidic (berries)	6 to 12 months
Fruit juices	6 to 9 months
Seafood (general)	1 year
Soups	1 year
Vegetables (general)	1 year
Vegetables (tomatoes, sauerkraut)	7 to 12 months

FATS AND OILS

Mayonnaise	2 months
Salad dressings	2 months
Salad Oil	6 to 9 months

GRAIN PRODUCTS

Cereal, to be cooked	8 months
Cereal, ready to eat	6 months
Flour	9 to 12 months
Macaroni	3 months
Mixes, prepared	6 months
Rice, parboiled	9 to 12 months
Rice, brown or wild	Should be refrigerated

SEASONINGS/SWEETENERS

Mustard, prepared	4 months
Salt	Indefinite
Spices	2 years to indefinite
Vinegar	2 years
Sugar/granulated & powdered	Indefinite
Brown Sugar	Should be refrigerated
Syrups	1 year

MISCELLANEOUS

Cookies/crackers	1 to 6 months
Dried fruits	6 to 8 months
Jams, jellies	Should be refrigerated
Nuts	1 year
Pickles	1 year
Potato chips	1 month

UNDERSTANDING LABELS

LABEL CLAIM	MUST MEAN
LOW FAT	A food with 3 grams of fat or less per serving. To make sure that this claim won't be made for high fat foods that are served in small portions, the food must also have 3 grams fat or less per 100 grams.
X % FAT FREE	The food is truly low in fat.
LIGHT, LITE	The food has one-third fewer calories than a comparable product. Other senses of "light"-for color, taste, or smell-must be clearly explained.
CHOLESTEROL FREE	One serving has less than 2 milligrams of cholesterol and 2 grams or less of saturated fat. The fat requirement insures that food with lots of fat from plant sources, like peanut butter, can no longer make this claim. Foods that never contain cholesterol-must underscore that fact, if they choose to make the claim.
LOW CALORIE	A food with fewer than 40 calories per serving and per 100 grams.
FRESH	The food is raw, not processed, frozen, or otherwise preserved.
HIGH IN...	One serving must provide 20% or more of the recommended daily intake for the stated nutrient. In the case of fiber claims, the label must declare the total fat content if a serving also packs more than 3 grams of fat.
A SOURCE OF...	Per serving, such a food must provide 10 to 19 percent of the daily quota for the stated nutrient.
LOW SODIUM	The food contains less than 140 milligrams per serving and per 100 grams. Foods claiming to be sodium free or salt free must contain less than 5 milligrams of sodium per serving.
(NUTRIENT)-FREE	The food contains a nutritionally trivial amount of the named nutrient.

NCS® M99491:321

Printed in U.S.A.

15

SAVE THE ENVIRONMENT - IT STARTS AT HOME

HINTS HINTS hints HINTS hints HINTS hints HINTS hints HINTS hints HINTS hints HINTS hints HINTS hints HINTS hints HINTS hints HINTS hints HINTS hints HINTS hints HINTS

Cleaning up the environment is the duty to all of us, one person recycling does make the difference.

* Buy products that can be recycled.
* Do not purchase over-packed products/or complain to the manufacturer.
* Buy products that are concentrated that can be diluted with water.
* Reuse paper bags/plastic bags when shopping.
* Buy non-toxic products.
* Monthly maintainance of changing furnace filters help keep the air clean.
* Purchase pump containers rather than aerosol dispensers.
* Purchase batteries that can be recharged.
* Use cloth diapers.
* Recycle old clothes be selling or donating.

PURCHASE PAPER PRODUCTS WITH THIS RECYCLING SYMBOL, INDICATES THAT THE ITEM IS MADE FROM RECYCLED PAPER.

PAPER PRODUCTS THAT ARE RECYCLABLE HAVE THIS SYMBOL.

PLASTICS CHART

HDPE

CODE	MATERIAL	EXAMPLES	MARKETS FOR THE RECYCLED MATERIALS
1	Polyethylene terephthalate (PET)	Soft drink bottles	Skis, surfboards, sailboat hulls, carpeting, fiberfill, paint brushes
2	High-density polyethylene (HDPE)	Milk, water jugs	Drain pipes, boat piers, traffic cones, signs, toys, flower pots, garden furniture, curb stops, portable toolboxes
3	Vinyl	Shampoo bottles	Truck bed inserts, industrial flooring.
4	Low-density polyethylene (LDPE)	Ketchup bottles	Mixed plastics: Insulation, office accessories
5	Polypropylene	Squeeze bottles	Park benches, fencing, car stops, boat docks
6	Polystyrene	Fast-food packaging	
7	Other		

WIDENER UNIVERSITY WOLFGRAM LIBRARY CHESTER, PA